RECOMMENDATIONS

Dr. Morey's speaking and writing ministry is recommended by some of the best-known Christian leaders in this generation.

Dr. D. James Kennedy
"Dr. Robert A. Morey is an excellent speaker and writer on the subject of cults and the occult, His books are excellent resource tools on these subjects. It is my pleasure to recommend him to churches everywhere throughout our land."

Dr. John Ankerberg
"I have known Dr. Robert Morey for a number of years and welcome this opportunity to recommend him to you. Dr. Morey is a man with an excellent understanding of the historic Christian faith and a particular skill as a defender of the Faith. I heartily recommend him to you."

Dr. Stephen Olford
"I praise the Lord that He has given you such a strategic ministry in the field of apologetics and theology. The Lord bless you richly."

Dr. Herbert Ehrenstein
"It is a genuine privilege for me to recommend Dr. Robert A. Morey as a competent Biblical scholar in the field of apologetics, Bible teaching and evangelism. I have known Dr. Morey for over 30 years and it has been a delight to me to see his developing a fantastic grasp of Biblical truth, and his unique ability to translate that exalted truth of God's Word into down-to-earth, meaningful and methodical ways his audiences can make use of it."

Dr. Kevin Johnson
"Dr. Robert Morey is one of the finest Biblical scholars in the field of comparative religious studies (apologetics) in North America. His books and presentations have been tremendously useful. I highly recommend him to you."

Death and The Afterlife

Nominated as "Book of the Year" by Cornerstone and chosen as "Best Reading" by Biblical Evangelist, this book quickly made it on several "Best Seller" lists. It has been featured on the John Ankerberg Show and many other radio/TV ministries. It has also been used in many seminaries such as Trinity Evangelical, Dallas, Southwestern, Conservative Baptist, Reformed, Gordon-Conwell, Moody Bible Institute, Southwestern, etc.

Dr. Roger Nicole (Reformed Seminary)

Dr. Morey's work provides an extensive examination of the biblical language related to human destiny beyond the grave. The lucid style and the very careful organization of the material make the work readily understandable to lay people as well as useful for pastors and other scholars.

Dr. Vernon Grounds (Conservative Baptist Seminary)

Since the earliest years of Christianity, the doctrine of eternal punishment has been fiercely attacked. Today that attack continues. Conditionalism and universalism are widely accepted as being biblically, logically and ethically far more acceptable than traditional theology. But Dr. Morey here presents a persuasive case with which anyone who seeks to malign or weaken the historical doctrine must reckon.

Dr. Jay Adams (Westminster Theological Seminary)

Here is a book to buy. It has been some time since a notable work on the future state of man after death has appeared. Morey's book admirably fills this gap. In addition to the Biblical data, as a plus, Morey includes a wealth of intertestamental and patristic resources.

Dr. Gleason Archer (Trinity Evangelical Divinity)

The author does everything right. His knowledge of the Jewish literature on death and the afterlife is profound. I recommend this work to one and all as the finest treatment of death, the soul, hell, and heaven.

Dr. Gary R. Habermas (Liberty University)

This volume generally exhibits a high degree of scholarship. One is repeatedly impressed by the amount of background material and research that had to be done in order to interact properly with the individual topics in Part I. This volume by Morey is a well-researched treatise on the biblical data concerning death and the afterlife. The topic of death and the afterlife is always a popular one. Accordingly, I recommend this book as a textbook for courses on cults or eschatology, whether for group studies or for personal reading. Much noteworthy data is supplied which needs to be studied and digested.

Christian Scholar's Review

Morey's book is the most comprehensive biblical study on the doctrine of death and the afterlife to appear in the last half century. He is a first-rate exegete whose command of the Hebrew and Greek languages is apparent in every chapter. He also displays a vast familiarity with the Apocrypha, Pseudepigrapha, Patristic material, Talmud, Midrash, Philo and Josephus. The author's careful scholarship and his attention to details make this volume a valuable contribution to the study of personal eschatology. Death and The Afterlife is a stimulating work worth reading.

Dr. Walter R. Martin (Christian Research Institute)

The first major work on the subject in this century, Death And The Afterlife will for many years be a standard reference work in this sorely neglected field. The scholarship of this volume will impress those who have studied the subject with any degree of thoroughness. At the same time, he communicates many great and profound truths in language that the average layman will both appreciate and profit from. It is a clear, cool breath of fresh air in the midst of a vacuum of doubt and unbelief.

John Ankerberg

A group of men have asked me to pick out what I consider to be the most important book on the market that Christians should read. The book I have chosen is Dr. Robert A. Morey's book, Death And The Afterlife. This is a landmark book that presents overwhelming proof for the biblical doctrine concerning death and the afterlife.

The Biblical Evangelist
	The jacket of this remarkable volume calls it "a landmark work." We are willing to go even further and describe it as "a masterpiece!" This book is especially devastating to the cultists and all those who teach soul sleep, annihilation and universalism. We urge every preacher and every Bible student to obtain a copy without delay!"

Spiritual Counterfeits Project
	Dr. Morey's book offers a source of order amidst the prevailing chaos of cultism, faddism, and quasi-Christian teaching about the subject of death and the afterlife. The section on exposition begins with a vitally necessary and helpful chapter "The Hermeneutics of Death." Here Dr. Morey present a brief but gutsy review of hermeneutical principles essential to a fair reading of Scripture. This chapter alone would make excellent required reading for Christian students. Students in my "Death, Dying, and Grieving" classes have also found Dr. Morey's discussion of the principle of progressive revelation significant in counseling Christians who wonder if the Old Testament presents views of death and the afterlife that contradict the New Testament. Dr. Morey's dual expertise in biblical languages and cult evangelism are combined to bring solid scholarship to bear on issues that affect not only scholars but the general populace, for as Dr. Morey insightfully notes, "the present popularity of the subject of death and the afterlife is extremely important to all of us, because the death rate is still one per person.

THE END OF THE WORLD ACCORDING TO JESUS

THE MT. OLIVET DISCOURSE
AND
THE BOOK OF REVELATION

By Dr. Robert A. Morey

PRESS

Copyright © 2010 by Dr. Robert A. Morey
Christian Scholars Press
P.O. Box 240
Millerstown, PA 17062
www.faithdefenders.com
1-800-41-TRUTH

The End of the World according to Jesus
by Dr. Robert A. Morey

Printed in the United States of America

ISBN 9781609571597

www.xulonpress.com

About the Author:
Dr. Robert Morey (B.A., M.Div., D. Min., Ph.D., D.D.) is an internationally recognized scholar in the fields of biblical philosophy, theology, and apologetics. He is the Executive Director of the Research and Education Foundation, which seeks to define, document, and defend "the faith once for all delivered unto the saints" (Jude 3). He has written over fifty books including:

The Bible, Natural Law, and Natural Theology: Conflict or Compromise?
A Bible Handbook on Slander and Gossip
Is Eastern Orthodoxy Christian?
The Islamic Invasion
Winning the War Against Radical Islam
The Trinity: Evidence and Issues
Death and The Afterlife
How the Old and New Testaments Relate to Each Other
The Nature and Extent of God's Knowledge
Fearing God
Studies in the Atonement
Battle of the Gods
Satan's Devices
The Encyclopedia of Practical Christianity
The Truth about Masons
How to Keep Your Faith While In College
The New Atheism and the Erosion of Freedom
An Introduction to Defending the Faith
When Is It Right To Fight?
How to Answer a Jehovah's Witness
How to Answer a Mormon
Reincarnation and Christianity
Horoscopes and the Christian
Worship Is Not Just For Sundays
How to Keep Your Kids Drug-Free
Here Is Your God
Is The Sabbath For Today?

Special thanks to Jon Powell and John Morey
for their help in preparing the manuscript.

Introduction

That the world had a Beginning and will have an End is one of the fundamental concepts of the Bible revealed from the first verse of Genesis to the last verse of the Apocalypse. Human history is like a train running on a predetermined track laid down in eternity by the Sovereign God who created it for His glory.

The train of history is rushing to a predetermined End when all the dead will be bodily resurrected in order to stand before King Messiah to be judged. He will declare the eternal destiny and condition of all men. A new heavens and a new earth will be created for the redeemed while the unregenerate face eternal conscious punishment in Hell. This is the truth the whole truth and nothing but the truth--according to the Holy Scriptures.

Most Christians believe in the End because the way the Bible is written. It begins at the Beginning and ends with the End. The prophets and apostles predicted that the world would one day End. King Messiah preached on the End so many times that He is called "The Apocalyptic Messiah." The final eternal condition of all men was *the* major theme of His teaching.[1]

It takes a great deal of energy and creativity to avoid and deny these fundamental truths. Yet, the cults and the occult have done so for centuries and, now for the first time, there are those who claim to be "Evangelical Christians" who openly deny the End of the world, the Day of Judgment, the Resurrection of the body, the eternal bliss of the elect, and the eternal conscious torment of the wicked.

In my debates with those who deny the doctrine of eternal conscious torment, I have always watched with amazement as they attempt to wiggle out the dozens of passages of Scripture that clearly speak of eternal torment. For example Rev. 14:9-11 says,

---

[1] Morey, Robert, *Death and the Afterlife*, (Millerstown:PA, Christian Scholars Press, 2009).

And another angel, a third one, followed them, saying with a loud voice, "If anyone worships the beast and his image, and receives a mark on his forehead or upon his hand, he also will drink of the wine of the wrath of God, which is mixed in full strength in the cup of His anger; and he will be tormented [βασανισθήσεται] with fire and brimstone in the presence of the holy angels and in the presence of the Lamb. And the smoke of their torment goes up forever and ever [εἰς αἰῶνας αἰώνων]; and they have no rest day and night [οὐκ ἔχουσιν ἀνάπαυσιν ἡμέρας καὶ νυκτὸς], those who worship the beast and his image, and whoever receives the mark of his name."

Dr. Erwin Lutzer of the Moody Church called me one day for advice on how best to debate Dr. Clark Pinnock, who openly denied the historic Evangelical doctrine of the eternal conscious punishment of unbelievers. They were going to debate this issue on the Moody radio network. I suggested that he immediately go to the above passage as soon as the debate began. Dr. Pinnock vainly tried to convince him that the word "torment" did not mean torment but no torment and that "forever and ever" did not mean forever and ever but only seconds! Dr. Lutzer won the debate with ease. Dr. Kistemaker's comment on Rev. 14:9-11 is clear.

The picture of torment is meant as a warning to the unbelievers, who in their daily lives reject the revelation of God and his Christ. John has taken the wording for this picture from the curse God pronounced on Edom, where pitch and sulfur will burn unquenched night and day while its smoke rises without ceasing (Isa. 34:9–10). God's archenemies are forever in the smoke of this fire that is tormenting them. There is no end to their

10

torment; they are unable to terminate it by death or annihilation (4 Macc. 13:15). It is impossible to escape God's righteous judgment except by repenting and believing in Christ during one's lifetime.

The Apocalypse is a book of contrasts from beginning to end. The smoke of the torment afflicting God's antagonists is the opposite of the smoke at the altar of incense mingled with the prayers of the saints that ascend to God (8:4). The clause "and they do not have rest day and night" refers to the wicked who suffer ceaselessly day and night in agonizing torment. This clause occurs also in the throne room scene, but there it refers to the four living creatures; they never stop singing, "Holy, holy, holy is the Lord God Almighty, who was, and is, and is to come" (4:8). While the wicked suffer, the cherubim sing praises to God. The worship of the beast leads to endless torment, but the worship of God to everlasting joy. [2]

In these dark days of apostasy all around us, it is good to be reminded that the biblical gospel is the clarion call to "flee from the wrath to come" (Mat. 3:7). Any so-called "gospel" that assures sinners there is no eternal wrath to flee is a false gospel and falls under the condemnation of Gal. 1:8. There is a heaven to gain and a hell to shun, just as surely as God exists!

The Mt. Olivet Discourse

As King Messiah approached the cross, He spoke what we now call the "Mt. Olivet Discourse." Matthew's account found in Matt. 24-25 is a summary of the teaching of the *earthly* Jesus on the End of the World. Matthew put together what Jesus said about

[2]Kistemaker, Simon J. ; Hendriksen, William: *New Testament Commentary : Exposition of the Book of Revelation.* Grand Rapids : Baker Book House, 1953-2001 (New Testament Commentary 20), S. 412

the End times during His entire ministry as well as what He said on Mt. of Olives. This is why Matthew's account is the passage of full mention on the earthy teaching of Messiah.

The Mt. Zion Discourse

After His death, burial, resurrection, and ascension, King Jesus revealed to the Apostle John what we call the "Book of Revelation." We must remember that the title of the book in the KJV "The Revelation of St. John the Divine" is erroneous because it contradicts the inspired title given in the first verse of the first chapter.

> The Revelation of Jesus Christ, which God gave Him to show to His bond-servants, the things which must shortly take place; and He sent and communicated *it* by His angel to His bond-servant John.

> Ἀποκάλυψις Ἰησοῦ Χριστοῦ ἣν ἔδωκεν αὐτῷ ὁ θεὸς δεῖξαι τοῖς δούλοις αὐτοῦ ἃ δεῖ γενέσθαι ἐν τάχει, καὶ ἐσήμανεν ἀποστείλας διὰ τοῦ ἀγγέλου αὐτοῦ τῷ δούλῳ αὐτοῦ Ἰωάννῃ

The title of the last book of the Bible is not "The Revelation of St. John the Divine" but "The Apocalypse of Messiah Jesus." Those who uphold the inspiration of the KJV have never been able to solve this obvious problem. Perhaps one reason why the KJV title was invented was the assumption that once Jesus sat down at the right hand of God the Father, this was the end of His teaching. But when Messiah ascended to heaven, this was not the *end* but the *beginning* of His mighty deeds and teachings. Dr. Luke in Acts 1:1 reminded us that the heavenly Jesus was *beginning* His work on earth.

> The first account I composed, Theophilus, about all that Jesus began to do and teach.

Τὸν μὲν πρῶτον λόγον ἐποιησάμην περὶ πάντων,
ὦ Θεόφιλε, ὧν ἤρξατο ὁ Ἰησοῦς ποιεῖν τε καὶ
διδάσκειν,

Dr. A. T. Robertson comment on this verse is very helpful.

Which Jesus began (*hôn êrxato Iêsous*)...Jesus
"began" "both to do and to teach" (*poiein te kai
didaskein*). Note present infinitives, linear action,
still going on, and the use of *te--kai* binds together
the life and teachings of Jesus, as if to say that Jesus
is still carrying on from heaven the work and
teaching of the disciples which he started while on
earth before his ascension. The record which Luke
now records is really the Acts of Jesus as much as
the Acts of the Apostles...The Acts, according to
Luke, is a continuation of the doings and teachings
of Jesus. "The following writings appear intended to
give us, and do, in fact, profess to give us, that
which Jesus *continued* to do and teach after the day
in which he was taken up" (Bernard, *Progress of
Doctrine in the N.T.*). [3]

In the last book of the Bible we have a record of Jesus'
"Mt. Zion Discourse" on the End of the World (Heb. 12:22). It is
the passage of full mention on the teaching of the *heavenly* Jesus
on the End of the world. When we put together the earthly and
heavenly teaching of Jesus on the end of the world, we have a
complete picture of what to expect as the train of human history
arrives at the End of the history. May God bless our study of these
two records of the teaching of Jesus on the End of the World.

3Robertson, A.T.: *Word Pictures in the New Testament*. Oak Harbor: Logos Research

Systems, 1997, S. Ac 1:1

Conclusion

Many pastors who attended the lecture series on the earthly and heavenly teaching of Jesus on the End of the World have requested that we retain the outline format of the material as it can be more easily preached to their congregation. For this practical reason, the outline format is retained without apology.

The Mt. Olivet Discourse

Table of Content

PART ONE:

PART TWO:

Preface

In the history of biblical interpretation, the Mt. Olivet Discourse has been the scene of far too much controversy. The passage has been abused by outrageous interpretations and has been misused by the cults as a pretext for their heresies, absurd teachings, and date setting. It is thus important for us to be humble enough to recognize that the passage is, in the words of Peter, "difficult to understand" (2 Pet. 3:16). Thus answers to some of our questions must await a personal interview with the Author in glory.

The most important step to take at the beginning of this study is to lay aside all our previous prejudices and interpretations and to step back and look at the Discourse as if this were the first time we are reading it. Don't approach the passage with an axe to grind or with a doctrine to prove. Approach it with an open mind to see what our Lord was saying to His disciples and to us.

I was sitting with Dr. Martin Lloyd Jones in London one day and I asked him how he studied   Scripture. He asked if I had the habit of underlining verses in my Bible or writing notes in the margin. I admitted that I did so. The first thing to do, he said, was to buy a version of the Bible that you never underline or write notes. The underlines and notes naturally lead your mind to repeat your previous ideas about the passage and prevent you from going any deeper. He read through a passage up to fifty times before he preached it. He was a very wise man.

In order to help you to approach the Discourse with an open mind and heart, we have put all three Gospel accounts of the Discourse in parallel columns so you can compare their different summaries of what Jesus said. Read the Gospel Parallel ten times before you begin to interpret it. Get out of the rut of old interpretations and ask the Spirit of God to open the passage anew to you.

Chapter One

Hermeneutics

The literary principles that guide your interpretation of Scripture in general should be applied to the Mt. Olivet Discourse in particular. There are *rules* that govern our interpretation of Scripture. Since I have explained this point in several books,[4] I will only briefly point out the key issues.

1. What are the different literary styles (genres) found in Scripture?
   A. historical narrative
   B. poetry
   C. conversations (direct and indirect)
   D. ethical imperatives
   E. legal codes (civil/religious/moral)
   F. worship (liturgy/music)
   G. apocalyptic (prophecy)
   H. theological discourse
   I. figurative language, metaphors, allegory, similes, etc.
   J. parables
   K. sarcasm, ridicule
   L. questions (sincere, rhetorical)

---

[4] See my books, *Death and the Afterlife* and *The Trinity* and my class syllabus on Hermeneutics for discussions on how to interpret the Bible (www.faithdefenders.com).

2. Each genre has its own unique set of literary principles of interpretation. Just as one shoe will not fit all feet, one hermeneutical principle will not fit all of Scripture.

Question: What significance does this hold for the hermeneutic that says that a passage must be interpreted *literally* unless there is something in the passage to indicate otherwise?

Answer: First, no one can define what the word "literal" means. For forty years I have asked for a clear definition, and have yet to receive one.

Second, whatever it means, no one in their right mind always interprets the Bible *literally*. Should we literally cut off our right hand and pluck out our right eye (Mat. 18:9)? Are we to literally "hate" our mother and father (Lk. 14:26)?

Third, if we applied a literalistic hermeneutic to Mal. 4:5-6, this would deny the Messianic claims of Jesus! There is nothing in Mal. 4:5-6 to indicate that Elijah would not *literally* show up and introduce the Messiah. The intertestamental Jews expected Elijah to ride out of heaven on a white horse to destroy the enemies of God and prepare the way for Messiah. But Jesus clearly stated that John the Baptist was spiritually the "Elijah" mentioned in Malachi (Matt. 11:14). John denied he was literally Elijah (John 1:21), and Luke simply said that John came in "the spirit and power of Elijah" (Lk. 1:17).

Question: What implication does this hold for the hermeneutic that a passage should be interpreted spiritually unless there is something in the context to indicate otherwise?

Answer: First, no one can define the word "spiritual."

Second, whatever it means, no one in their right mind always interprets the Bible *spiritually*. The early Christians literally followed the command of Jesus to flee the city of Jerusalem (Matt. 24:16) and not one Christian perished when Titus destroyed the city.

Third, a spiritualistic hermeneutic applied to Num. 24:17 would destroy the fulfillment of prophecy concerning the birth of Messiah. Who would ever think that Num. 24:17 meant a *literal* star?

The key is to realize that one principle of interpretation cannot interpret all of Scripture. To attempt to do so is to commit the fallacy of reductionism and twist Scripture beyond recognition.

3. If you confuse genres and apply the wrong principle of interpretation to a passage, you will end up with a false interpretation. For example, if you interpret the Psalms in the same way that you interpret the Book of Acts, you will end up with absurd interpretations. Is God really a dragon with smoke coming out of his nose and fire out of his mouth (Psa. 18:8)?

4. The most frequent mistake of interpretation today is to forget that the Bible is a collection of sixty six ancient Jewish scrolls that must be understood in terms of their unique Jewish literary and cultural context. Any verse taken out of context becomes a pretext for heresy.

5. The Bible is not the product of Western European literary traditions and the attempt to force the Jewish Scriptures into Western European literary principles has been the mother of many heresies. One modern example is Joseph Campbell, who applies his modern Western concepts of myth, saga, and legend to the Bible. His literary principles were unknown in biblical times and are Gentile - not Jewish, modern - not ancient, etc.

The New Testament as a Whole

The structure of the New Testament as a whole is the context of the Mt. Olivet Discourse.

Book	How it relates to Messiah
Matthew, Mark, Luke, John	Manifestation
Acts	Proclamation
Romans-Philemon	Explanation
Hebrews-Jude	Application
Revelation	Expectation

The four Gospels record what Messiah said and did up to His ascension to the right hand of the Father in heaven. The Book of Acts records the apostle's proclamation of the person and work of Messiah to the Jews and Gentiles and how the early Church began and spread throughout the world. The Church Epistles explain the theological implications of what Messiah said and did according to the preaching of the apostles. The General Epistles apply the theology of Messiah to the daily life of the believer. The Book of the Apocalypse explains what will take place before, during, and after Messiah returns to establish His kingdom on earth.

The abuse of these observations by ultra-dispensationalists does not negate the validity of the literary structure of the New Testament. The general structure of the New Testament is not to be taken in an absolute sense in which there are no exceptions to it. For example, a Gospel writer may break into his narrative and explain to his readers what is happening or what was said. The following texts are biblical examples of where Gospel writers broke into their narrative to explain what was going on: Mat. 2:15, 17, 23; 4:14; 24:15; Mk. 6:31; 7:3-4, 11, 19; Lk. 2:23; 8:8; 16:14; 23:50-51; John 1:41; 2:9; Acts 17:21. A. T. Robertson points out in his comments on Matt. 24:15.

> Let him that readeth understand (ho anaginoskôn noeitô). This parenthesis occurs also in Mr 13:14. It is not to be supposed that Jesus used these words.

22

They were inserted by Mark as he wrote his book
and he was followed by Matthew.

The literary structure of the New Testament means that we should not depend solely on historical narratives or poetry as the basis of our theology. If the only verses you have to support a doctrine comes from poetry or historical narrative, this should count as a reason *not* to believe that doctrine.

The Book of Matthew

The Gospel of Matthew is a *historical narrative* of the birth, life, teachings, death, and resurrection of the Messiah. What does this mean? This means that it should not be used as the *primary* or *sole* foundation of your theology because historical narratives merely record what happened, where and when it happened, who was there, who did what to whom, what was said, etc. By their literary nature, historical narratives simply record what happened. They do not usually explain them. Why? Experience does not carry within itself its own interpretation. The interpretation must come from outside of the experience.

Question: What implication does this hold for those theological systems that base their teachings *primarily* on Matthew's summary of the Mt. Olivet discourse? Answer: Preterism is the heresy that all prophecy was fulfilled at and by the destruction of the Temple in A.D. 70. Thus the Second Coming of Christ, the Resurrection, the Judgment, etc. are not future events *before* us but past events *behind* us. They use Matt. 24 as the primary basis of their hermeneutic and doctrine. Thus the methodology that underlies their theology is erroneous.

Secondly, Matthew summarized a question/answer session between the disciples and Jesus that took place on the Mount of Olives. It was thus not a sermon or discourse *per se* but a dialogue or two way discussion.

Thirdly, Matthew adds to the dialogue other material that Jesus gave elsewhere. This gives us additional problems and challenges when attempting to interpret it.

1. Each Gospel writer summarized the sermons, parables, and discussions of Jesus in his own words. Thus we do not have a "word for word" transcript of the actual words of Jesus except for a catchy phrase here or there. There were no audio recorders in those days!
2. Some editions of the New Testament put the "words" of Jesus in red. This gives people the false idea that we have a "word for word" transcript of the words of Jesus. This is not true and we suggest that you do not use red-letter editions of the NT.
3. The false assumption that we have word-for-word transcripts of what Jesus said has led skeptics to point out many *apparent* contradictions in the Bible. When you compare the Gospel accounts on the sermons, parables and prayers of Jesus, they have different wording. The Lord's Prayer and the signs over the cross (at Jesus' crucifixion?) are good examples of this.

   Each Gospel writer summarized the sermons, parables, and prayers of Jesus in his own words and in such a way as to answer his unique question. He selected material from the life and teaching of Messiah that relates to that question.

Gospel Name	Main Question Answered	Intended Audience	Recorded Audience	Recorded Location
Matthew	What did Jesus say?	Jews	Crowds in public	Galilee
Mark	What did Jesus do?	Romans	Crowds in public	Galilee
Luke	Who followed Jesus?	Greeks	Crowds in public	Galilee
John	Who was Jesus?	Christians	Disciples in private	Judea

4.

    a. Matthew answered the question: What did Jesus say? It is thus no surprise to find that the fullest account of what Jesus said is in Matthew. Indeed, if you cut out of the book of Matthew all the sermons, parables, sayings, etc. of Jesus, there would be nothing left! His record of the Sermon on the Mount, the parables, prayers, and discourses of Jesus should be given the priority when studying the teachings of Jesus.

    b. Mark answered the question: What did Jesus do? The key words are "immediately", "power", etc. If the mighty deeds of Jesus were removed from the book of Mark, there would be nothing left. He was interested in the works of Jesus- not His words. Since his audience was Gentile, he was not interested in *Jewish* things such as genealogies, the virgin birth, Old Testament prophecies, etc.

    c. Luke answered the question: Who followed Jesus? He is the only Gospel writer who gives us little biographies of people like Simeon and Anna that the other Gospel writers do not mention. Whenever possible, he interviewed the people involved and asked them about their inner thoughts and feelings while they were with Jesus. For example, he tells us what went through the mind of Mary when the angel told her she would become pregnant with the Messiah. He asked her and she told him what she felt.

    d. John answered the question: Who was Jesus? This is why the writer who records the "I am" statements of Jesus such as "I am" the good shepherd, the door, the light of the world, the bread from heaven, the Vine, etc. It is thus no wonder that John is the writer who records where Jesus is explicitly called God and worshipped as God (John 1:1, 18; 20:28).

5.   Each Gospel writer summarized the sermons, parables and prayers of Jesus with their target audience in mind.

   a. The audience of Matthew: Jews.
   b. The audience of Mark: Romans.
   c The audience of Luke: Greeks
   d. The audience of John: Christians

6.   One example of this is that Matthew, in deference to the Jews who were superstitious about using the word "God," used "kingdom of *heaven*" in his record of the same parables for which both Mark and Luke used "kingdom of *God.*" The failure to understand this led some people to think there were two different kingdoms!

7.   There are no *real* contradictions between Matthew, Mark, and Luke. When you put them together, you get the whole picture.

8.   The Mt. Olivet Discourse must be reconstructed by putting together the three accounts found in Matthew, Mark, and Luke. If you fail to compare the three synoptic Gospels and rely only on Matthew's summary, you will not be able to understand what Jesus said. For example, Matthew only records *three* questions that Jesus was asked while a comparison of all three Gospel accounts reveals that the disciples actually asked *four* questions.

I will never forget the old preacher who attended the first seminar on the Mt. Olivet Discourse. When I said that Jesus was asked *four* questions, he raised his hand and "corrected" me that there were only *three* questions. I asked him if he had ever compared side by side the three Gospels on the Discourse, he admitted that he had never done that. He had preached only on

26

Matt. 24 for 40 years and never compared it with Mark and Luke. I took him to the other two accounts and proved to him that the disciples asked four questions!

9. John does not record the Mt. Olivet Discourse because he dealt with what Jesus did and said while in Judea with his disciples in private. The Synoptic Gospels record what Jesus did and said in Galilee with the crowds in public.

Thirdly, the Mt. Olivet Discourse is *Jewish Apocalyptic literature* and thus it requires a third layer of interpretation. If you only read Matt. 24 you will miss point. Luke 17:30 uses the word ἀποκαλύπτω in the Greek text. Thus the *apocalyptic* nature of the Discourse cannot be denied.

It will be just the same on the day that the Son of Man is revealed.
(Luke 17:30)
κατὰ τὰ αὐτὰ ἔσται ᾗ ἡμέρᾳ ὁ υἱὸς τοῦ ἀνθρώπου ἀποκαλύ πτεται.

The classic commentators state,

ἀποκαλύπτεται .   A technical expression in this connexion (1 Cor. 1:7; 2 Thes. 1:7; 1 Pet. 1:7, 13, 4:13). The present tense indicates the certainty of the veil being withdrawn. Up to that day He is hidden from man's sight: then at once He is revealed. [5]

The use of ἀποκαλύπτεται corresponds exactly to Mt. παρουσία (cf. 1 Cor. 1:7; 2 Thes. 1:7; 1 Pet. 1:7,

---

[5] Plummer, Alfred: A Critical and Exegetical Commentary on the Gospel According to S. Luke. London : T &T Clark International, 1896, S. 408

13; 4:13), and is probably original (*pace* Schulz, 280). [6]

A Brief Introduction to Jewish Apocalyptic Writings

1. Jewish apocalyptic literature is a unique genre of ancient Middle Eastern literature and was unknown in Western Europe. Since we will give a detailed analysis of this kind of literature in Part Two in our introduction to the Book of Revelation, we will only give a brief overview of this subject here. We should interpret the Mt. Olivet Discourse in the same way that other apocalyptic literature was interpreted by the Jews during the inter-testamental period between Malachi and Matthew.

2. The Old Testament background of the vocabulary and figures of speech must be studied carefully. Standard Greek NT editions will indicate any OT citations or allusions in the passage.

3. The inter-testamental apocalyptical literature provides some helpful insights. Both Charles and Charlesworth (see bibliography) should be consulted for literary parallels.

4. The New Testament Psuedepigrapha should also be consulted to see example of the apocalyptic literature produced by the early Palestinian Church.

5. One example of the apocalyptic hermeneutical principle is that the events clustered around the End Times do not have a fixed order or chronology. Since no one knows the exact details of how they will happen, they were arranged and then rearranged in different orders by the same author to emphasize different aspects of the End. The Jews understood that since no one knew the exact chronology of events at the End, different chronologies could be given by the same author. Western hermeneutics would view different orders or chronologies as contradictory. This is

why liberals identify different chronologies as contradictions in the Bible. Their ignorance of ancient Jewish writings is the root cause of their failure to understand the Bible.

6. One clear example of Jesus using the Jewish apocalyptic hermeneutic is found in a comparison between Matt. 13:39-43 and Matt. 24:31. In Mat. 13, at the End, the angels will take away (rapture) the unbelievers and the believers are left behind. Yet, in Matt. 24:31, the angels take away (rapture) the believers and the unbelievers are left behind. The order is reversed by Jesus. Atheists and skeptics have used these two passages to prove (sic) that Jesus contradicted himself and hence could not be God incarnate. They only reveal their ignorance of how ancient Jewish literature was written.

7. The first evidence of Preterism in early Jewish writings is found in two apostate Jews, Josephus and Philo. Both of them had abandoned Judaism and adopted Platonic Greek philosophy in its place. It is thus no wonder that they both taught that the "abomination of desolation" predicted in Dan. 9:27; 11:31, and 12:11 had already been fulfilled by Antiochus Epiphanes who erected an altar to Zeus on the altar of Jehovah (1Macc. 1:54, 59; 6:7; 2Macc. 6:1-5). The apocalyptic Jews saw Daniel's prophecy as yet unfilled.

Did Jesus side with the Preterists or with the apocalyptic Jews? A. T. Robertson points out,

> Jesus makes an allusion to Dan. 9:27; 11:31; 12:11...The desolation in the mind of Jesus is apparently the Roman army (Luke 21:20) in the temple, an application of the words of Daniel to this dread event...Josephus tells us that the Romans burned the temple and offered sacrifices to their ensigns placed by the eastern gate when they proclaimed Titus as Emperor.[7]

7Robertson, A.T.: Word Pictures in the New Testament. Oak Harbor : Logos Research Systems, 1997, S. Mt 24:15

Jesus clearly rejected the Preterist interpretation of Daniel and clearly taught the futurist position.

8. Another apocalyptic hermeneutical principle is that God prepared mankind to understand the End by giving us "previews" throughout redemptive history. Thus the Flood, the destruction of Sodom, the judgment of the Canaanites, the Captivities, droughts, locust plagues, the destruction of the temple in A.D. 70, etc. are described using End language and figures of speech in order for them to function as "previews of coming attractions."

We must not confuse the End with the previews. For example, apocalyptic language was used to describe the Flood (Jude 1:14-15). Just because the Flood was described in the language of the End, it would be a mistake to reduce the End to the Flood.

9. This insight reveals another major error of Preterism. They assume that since the destruction of the temple was described by Jesus with apocalyptic language this means it was the End of the world. But Pentecost was described by Peter with apocalyptic language (Acts 2:16-20) and this took place before the destruction of the temple.

10. In apocalyptic literature, the End is visualized using things from the contemporary life-experience of the author. This is why the final triumph of good over evil at the End of history is pictured in terms of a rebuilt Jewish temple complete with priests, animal sacrifices, incense, bells, etc. Gentiles will grab the robes of Jews to follow them to Jerusalem to participate in temple worship. How else could a Jew under the Old Covenant visualize it? All he knew was the trappings of Old Covenant worship.

11. Some Western Christians, not understanding the nature of apocalyptic language, have argued that in the millennium the Old Covenant with all its shadows would be reinstated. But the Book of Hebrews clearly teaches that the New Covenant has replaced the Old Covenant because it was defective and only a shadow of the New. Now that *the* Lamb has died, no more

30

lambs need die. The Old Covenant with its priesthood, animal sacrifices, food codes, high priest, etc. is forever gone. Because the Old Covenant was only "temporary," the New Covenant is called the "eternal" covenant (Heb. 13:20).

12. The final Battle between good and evil is pictured in terms of the battles, weapons, garments, animals, and nations of the day in which it was written. What implication does this hold for those who believe that Armageddon will be literally waged with men on horses using swords and spears or that Jesus will literally ride out of heaven on a literal white horse? It renders such interpretations total nonsense.

Modern dispensationalists have given up their claim that the final battle will on horseback and now admit that tanks and airplanes would be the proper interpretation. But I remember them counting how many horses could be found in Russia and China because they demanded horses be used in Armageddon!

13. The eternal state is visualized with images drawn from the life experience of the author. Each author pictured it in different ways. This is not contradiction, but apocalyptic. For example, will we literally sit under a fig tree for eternity while watching children play with poisonous snakes (Micah 4:4; Isa. 11:8)?

14. Both heaven and hell are described with apocalyptic language. Since the final state of the righteous and the wicked do not yet exist, mixed metaphors are allowed in their apocalyptic descriptions.

15. Hell is described as a lake of fire, the mist of darkness, a garbage dump with worms and smoldering fires, etc. without contradiction. This is the major error of the heresies of soul sleep and annihilationism.[8] They make literal what was only intended to be metaphorical. The fire of hell is a symbol of the anger of God that abides on the damned for all eternity. It is not a literal fire that literally burns up the wicked and reduces them to literally nothing.

---

[8] See my book, *Death and the Afterlife,* for my discussion on hell and heaven (www.faithdefenders.com).

16. Heaven can be described with mixed metaphors without contradiction. In biblical times, gold, silver, and precious stones were the most valuable items in life. Is it any wonder that heaven was pictured with streets paved with gold, gates made of pearl, walls studded with precious stones, etc.? In cultures where those things are not valued, heaven would be pictured differently.

17. I know it will distress some people to learn that heaven does not literal streets paved with literal gold or literal jewel encrusted walls, pearl gates, fish fries or pets. Others will get upset that there are no literal mansions in heaven. But their expectations are not biblical. Since the *souls* of believers go to heaven at death while their bodies rest in the grave awaiting the Resurrection (2 Cor. 5:1-9) and since souls are immaterial and invisible, they do not need houses, clothing or streets, fish fries, pets, etc. The white robes are symbolic of the righteousness of Christ imputed to believers in justification and not literal robes. Spirits and souls could not wear a robe even if they wanted to. Some Christians foolishly think that they will stand around in white choir robes singing hymns for all eternity. How boring!

Conclusion

Apocalyptic hermeneutics should change the way you approach Bible prophecy in general, and the Mt. Olivet Discourse and Book of Revelation in particular.

Chapter Two

The Life of Messiah

First, in terms of a chronology of the life of Messiah, when did the Mt. Olivet Discourse take place? The discourse took place on the Tuesday evening of "Passion Week" that led up to His crucifixion. It was the last recorded "bull session" of Messiah with His disciples before his death.

Second, Matthew used the 1st century rabbinic technique of "clustering" or grouping of material by which he gathered together the sayings, miracles, parables, and discourses of Messiah, irrespective of when, where or to whom they were delivered and arranged topically. For example, he gathered together all the "Kingdom" parables that Jesus gave at different times and places and "clustered" them together in chapter 13. This why the other Gospel writers placed then elsewhere in terms of chronology. Lenski comments,

> Matthew handles this material with complete mastery. He is not fettered by chronology considerations, as an ordinary historian. While he follows the general chronological order as given by the life of Jesus he, nevertheless, groups some details according to their character and significance.[9]

Third, given his Jewish audience, Matthew carefully compared Moses and Messiah in his Gospel.

---

[9] Lenski, R. C., Matthre, p. 20

Comparing Moses & Jesus

Who	Went up on a mountain and brought down the	Gave new commandments to	Teachings arranged in five	Miraculously fed the multitude in the wilderness
Moses	Old Covenant	Israel	Books	Yes
Jesus	New Covenant	The Church	Discourses	Yes

- Moses went up a mountain and brought down the Old Covenant.
  Jesus went up a mountain and brought down the New Covenant.

- Moses gave Israel new commandments.
  Jesus gave the Church new commandments.

- Moses' teachings were arranged in five books.
  Jesus' teachings were arranged in five discourses.

- Moses miraculously fed the multitude in the wilderness.
  Jesus miraculously fed the multitude in the wilderness.

Since John's audience was Christians, he contrasted Moses and Messiah and emphasized that Messiah was God (John 1:17-18).

Four, Matthew arranged the material in the following literary pattern.

Narrative 1:1-4:25

1st Discourse 5:1-7:29

Narrative 8:1-9:34
2nd Discourse 9:35-10:42

Narrative 11:1-12:50
3rd Discourse 13:1-52

Narrative 13:53-17:27
4th Discourse 18:1-35

Narrative 19:1-22:46
5th Discourse 23:1-25:46

Narrative 26:1-28:20

Fifth, when Matthew rearranged the life and teachings of Messiah into clusters, he often did so in groups of three.

- Christ's genealogy was arranged into three sections.
- The magi gave the infant Jesus three gifts.
- Satan tempted Jesus three times.
- A woman hid three pecks of meal.
- The multitude listened to Jesus for three days.
- The disciples built three tabernacles.
- Peter denied the Lord three times.
- Jesus picked three disciples to be with him.
- Matthew records three groupings of three kinds of miracles.
- Three illustration of righteousness.
- Three prohibitions.
- Three commands.
- Three prayers.
  etc.

One possible reason why Matthew put three things together in a cluster is that he wanted to emphasize that Jesus had three "witnesses" (cf. Deut. 19:15) that backed up His claims and teachings.

Six, we must emphasize that Matthew did not invent the three things he clustered together. They were not fictional, but factual. He merely selected three things that Jesus said or did during His lifetime and arranged them into a cluster of three as a witness to the claims of Messiah.

Conclusion

The Mt. Olivet Discourse must be seen in its place in the chronology of the life and death of Messiah. As He approached the end of His life, He answered questions about the end of all life. Moses' covenant was coming to an end as the new covenant was inaugurated at the Last Supper. The end of temple worship with all its trappings of animal sacrifices, priests, bells, and incense were coming to an end with the self-sacrifice of the Lamb of God upon the altar of the cross. The Old Testament prophecy of the priesthood of all believers was about to be fulfilled.

Chapter Three

The Historical Setting

The historical and cultural contexts will supply us with the "who, what, where, when, why, and how" of the Matt 24-25? Discourse, bringing the hermeneutical lens into clearer focus. Consult all three synoptic accounts to discover the various contexts.

First, what was the *political* context that initially provoked the discourse? Herod's Temple represented Rome's conquest of and rule over Israel. It was indeed "Herod's" temple and not Yahweh's, as it was a symbol of his sell-out to Rome. It was a pathetic attempt to reproduce Solomon's Temple on a much smaller and less grand scale. It represented the power and glory of Rome as well as King Herod.

Just as its building represented the beginning of Rome's rule over Israel, its destruction could only mean the *end* of Rome's rule. The geo-politics of the situation must be understood to appreciate the psychological impact of Messiah's prediction that "not one stone would be left upon another." That the disciples jumped to the false conclusion that the "end" of the temple somehow meant the End of the world is understandable in this light.

Second, what was the *immediate situation* that provoked the disciples to ask Jesus questions? Jesus and the disciples had just left the Temple where He had once again created controversy. We must remember that Jesus began His ministry by first coming to the outer court of the temple and denouncing the money changers as thieves. He drove them out with violence. Now, at the end of His ministry, He visits the temple again and this time denounces the Pharisees and Scribes as hypocrites!

There is no record of Jesus participating in any temple worship ceremonies during His ministry. The Essenes and many other Jewish sects rejected Herod's temple and did not participate in temple worship.

Once Jesus and his disciples had escaped the chaos at the temple, they retired to the seclusion of Mt. Olivet where they could ask Jesus in private what He meant when He said that not one stone would be left on another. If they would have asked Him publicly while in the temple, it would have created more tension with the leaders of the temple.

Third, while in the temple, the disciples were clearly in awe of the display of wealth and power in the temple architecture. When they pointed out to Jesus the stones in the walls of the temple, Jesus shocked them by predicting that the temple would be destroyed and that not one stone would be left on top of another. As a result, they could not stop thinking about what He said to them and as soon as they were alone with Him, they asked Him what He meant.

Fourth, why did they link the destruction of the temple to the End of the world? The disciples were confused about many things. They assumed that Messiah would liberate Israel from Rome. Once the Romans were driven out of Israel, they would sit on thrones ruling the nation as kings under the King of Kings. They assumed that Herod's temple would the center of the worship of the new Israel.

This is why we are told that they could not understand what Jesus was talking about when He said that He was going up to Jerusalem to die. In their expectations, He was to reign as an earthly king, not die on a cross as a common criminal. Even after His resurrection, they still hoped that He was going to liberate Israel from Rome and establish His own earthly kingdom with them sitting on thrones (Acts 1:6).

Now that Jesus said He was going to die and that the temple would be destroyed, these two things could only mean things were not going to turn out as the disciples hoped. They confused the end of the temple with the End of the world.

Preterism is also based on this same false assumption. The Preterists convolute the two events into one event.

Fifth, the *psychological condition* of the disciples is important. They were experiencing dismay, shock, and disappointment. They had assumed that they would all have high placed jobs in Messiah's kingdom once He drove the Romans away. They even argued over who would sit on the thrones on the right and left of His throne. The mother of James and John tried to manipulate her sons into those positions.

Sixth, these same psychological factors help us to understand Judas' decision to betray Jesus and the subsequent depression that led to his suicide. John tells us that Jesus knew from the beginning that Judas did not really believe. Judas hoped to ride Jesus' coattails to glory in the coming kingdom (John 6:64). Judas wiggled his way into being the money keeper for the group so he could steal it (John 12:4-6). Judas probably rationalized his theft of ministry funds by thinking that he "deserved" the money for his time and trouble for volunteering to help Jesus

Judas was the only disciple who clearly understood what Jesus meant when He said that He was going to Jerusalem to die. Jesus was not going to Jerusalem to be crowned King! It was thus time for Judas to "get out of Dodge." By leaving at this point, Judas would accomplish two things. First, he could avoid getting killed with Jesus. Second, he could get some money out the deal by selling out Jesus to the Pharisees. In his mind, he "deserved" more money for all the time and effort he had wasted on the ministry of Jesus. After all, Jesus had betrayed him first by not becoming king and giving him a high position in his kingdom.

The depression that drove Judas to suicide was to be expected, because we can lie to ourselves only so much. He tried to justify his betrayal of Jesus by thinking that Jesus had betrayed him first. Failed expectations and violated rights allow the cancer of bitterness to grow and fester in the heart. But, in the end, when no one was around, Judas knew deep down that Jesus never betrayed him and that Jesus never did him any harm. Judas knew he was a thief and a liar, and there was no way to justify his betraying Jesus.

Once he threw the thirty pieces of silver at the feet of the Pharisees, he thought this would undo his wicked betrayal of Jesus. But his depression only grew deeper. This led him to "end it all" by hanging himself.

Conclusion

The above help us to recreate the emotionally charged setting of the question and answer session on Mt. Olivet. It was not a cold academic discussion of Bible prophecy but an intense emotional discussion of the future of Jesus, the temple, the nation, the Romans and their hopes for a good job and glory in an earthly kingdom.

Chapter Four

The Four Questions

As they sat on Mt. Olivet, overlooking the temple, the disciples thought about what Jesus said about it being destroyed completely. Four of the disciples approached Jesus with questions. Since there were four disciples who approached Jesus, it should not surprise us that there were four different questions, one from each disciple. The second question was phrased in two different ways. By using the Gospel parallel, the four questions are:

1. "When will these things take place?"
2. "What will be the sign when these things will be put into place?" (Mk)
   "What will be the sign that these things are about to take place?" (Lk)
3. "What will be the sign of your coming?"
4. "What will be the sign of the end of the age?"

Why Matthew Only Recorded Three Questions

First, some Christians have been confused by Matthew's recording only three of the four questions. Given the fact that Matthew liked to cluster things in groups of three, that he would only record three of the four questions is just another example of the way he arranged his Gospel material in triads.[10]

Second, the four questions can be arranged in a chiastic structure.

----

[10] This is pointed out by Guthrie in his N.T. Introduction (I:27-31).

1. When will these things take place (be)?

2. What will be the sign when these things are about to take place?

3. What will be the sign of your coming?

4. What will be the sign of the end of the age?

The chiastic structure of the four questions reveal that the first two questions have the destruction of the temple in view while the third and fourth questions have the "end of the age" and the 2nd "Coming" of Messiah in view.

Fourth, the words "these things" are the focus of the first question. The context is absolutely clear that "these things" in the first question referred to the destruction of the temple. This means is that any interpretation of the Discourse that assumes that all four questions refer only to the destruction of the temple (Preterism) or to the end of the age (Dispensationalism) is erroneous.

The immediate concern of the first disciple was Jesus' prediction of the destruction of the temple. He wanted Jesus to give him a specific time or date for it. But Jesus never got involved in date setting for the destruction of the temple or the end of the age. As we shall see, He never answered the first question.

Fifth, the second question goes beyond the first question and asks what will be the "sign" that "these things" were about to happen. The 2nd disciple accepted the fact that "these things" (the destruction of the temple) was going to happen. His question focused on how to prepare himself for that event by Jesus giving a clear "sign" (i.e. event) that would be easy to recognize so he and others could react immediately.

Did Jesus give him a clear-cut sign that would be easily recognized? History records that when Jerusalem and its temple were destroyed by Titus not one Christian perished. They had all fled to the hills and escaped the bloodbath. Why did they flee to the mountains? Dr. Luke gives us the answer. Jesus told the disciple,

> When you see Jerusalem surrounded by armies, then understand that is devastation is near. Then those in Judea must flee to the mountains, those inside the city must leave it, and those in the countryside must no go into it. (Lk. 21:20-21)

Both Matthew and Mark go on to record that Jesus warned that this will be difficult for those who are pregnant or who recently gave birth. But they must act immediately without delay when the armies approach the city. People should not even back to the house to grab a coat or pack possessions. They should drop whatever they are doing at the time and run for the hills as fast as their feet could carry them. Since there was a ban on traveling on the Sabbath, they must pray that the armies will not show up on the Sabbath (Matt. 24:15-22 cf. Mk. 13:14-20 cf. Lk. 21:20-24).

Stop and think about it. Jesus gave a specific answer that could not be misunderstood. When they saw the armies of Rome approaching the city they must flee at once. The Christians all understood this clearly and they all, without exception, ran away as the armies approached. Thus history records that not one Christian died when Titus destroyed the city, demolished the temple stone by stone, and either killed or enslaved the inhabitants.

Sixth, the disciples now understood what was going to happen to the temple and how to prepare for it. But some of them, if not all of them, wrongly assumed that such a national and religious disaster as the destruction of Jerusalem and its temple could only mean the end of the world as they knew it.

We must emphasize that they were not thinking about the end of the planet but of the "age" of Gentile domination over Israel. The Jews looked beyond the age of the Gentile to the age of Messiah. In the Babylonian Talmud some rabbis even predicted how many years each age would last. [11]

Questions three and four revealed that the disciples falsely assumed that the end of the temple meant the end of the age. Then they compounded the error by also wrongly assuming that the end

---

[11] See the appendix in *Death and the Afterlife* on the Misnah and Talmud.

of the age meant the triumphant "coming" of the Messiah to drive the Gentiles out of Israel and usher in the Messianic kingdom.

Seventh, ancient Jewish and modern Western literary traditions are not only different but opposite of each other at times. For example, Europeans and Americans read and write from left to right while Jews read and write from right to left. This insight helps us understand the difference between modern Gentiles and ancient Jews when in comes to the order in which you answer questions.

When a European or American is asked several questions, he or she will answer them in the order in which they were asked. They were taught to do this in elementary school. It is thus no surprise that most Western commentators assume that Jesus answered the four questions in the order in which they were given, i.e. Jesus answered the 1st question in the 1st section of the Discourse and so forth. This has led to much confusion and frustration because the Discourse is not structured that way. Instead, Jesus followed the rabbinic method of answering the last question first and working back to the third question and then second question.

I will never forget the young pastor who came up to me during a break in the seminar. His face was aglow with the epiphany that he had read the Discourse with the wrong order in mind. He explained, "I was always afraid to preach on the Mt. Olivet Discourse because I did not see where Jesus answered the questions in the order in which they were given. Now, I see that He began with the last question and worked back to the other question, I finally understand what He was saying and I can now preach it to my people."

Eight, notice the key words in each question:

When will *these things* take place?
What will be *the sign* that these things are about to take place?
What will be the sign of your *coming*?
What will be the sign of *the end* of the age?

44

The key words in the 4th question are "the end." If Jesus began answering that question first, when we would expect to find the words "the end" to appear. But if Jesus began with the 1st question, then we would expect to find the words "these things" in the first section of the Discourse.

If you examine the Gospel Parallel, you will find that Jesus began with a discussion concerning "the end," not "these things." Then as you trace the usage of all the key words, you will see that Jesus answered the questions starting with the fourth, to the third, to the second question. Why did Jesus ignore the first question?

Ninth, the first question focused on "*When* will these things take place," i.e. they wanted Jesus to set a date for the destruction of the temple. But Jesus never answered "when" questions. For example, how did Jesus deal with the "when" question in Acts 1:6-7? He refused to set any dates whatsoever and reminded the disciples that the future was in the hands of God *alone* and that their responsibility was to spread the Gospel, not speculate about the future.

In this light, it should not surprise us that Jesus went out His way during His Discourse to emphasize that no one knows the "when" of the End (Mat. 24:36, 42-44; Mk. 13:32-37). Jesus had no problem dealing with "What" questions, such as questions two, three, and four. The "what" had to do with "signs" that would indicate that the events predicted were beginning to take place.

Tenth, since some of the disciples would be alive when the temple was destroyed, Jesus gave clear specific "signs" so they could have time to run away. Thus any "signs" that were readily identifiable would relate to the destruction of the city and temple that took place in A.D. 70. *The closer the fulfillment, the clearer the signs.*

Eleventh, since the "Coming" and the "End" were thousands of years off, none of the disciples would live to see it. Thus Jesus was vague about the details surrounding the Coming and the End. *The further away the fulfillment, the vaguer the signs.*

These two insights help us to understand Mat. 24:34; Mk. 13:30; Lk. 21:32.

Thirteenth, the proper interpretation of the Discourse is further complicated because Jesus would get off topic and go a tangent issue such as the need for watchfulness, patience, etc. (ex. Matt. 24:42, etc.) These tangents have to be put aside when studying the prophetic material.

Fourteenth, this is why some verses are "out of order" according to modern Western standards. We must remember that Jesus was not giving a formal lecture but was in an informal private discussion or "bull session" with His disciples. It took place in real life and involved give and take. Thus it is not surprising that Jesus would start out discussing one question and then jump other to another question and then go back to the original question and then go off on a tangent.

Fifteenth, since the material found in Matt. 25 does not appear in Mark's or Luke's record of the Olivet Discourse, it was probably not part of the original Mt. Olivet discourse. Why do we say this?

In writing his Gospel, Matthew used a rabbinic technique called "clustering" in which, when he encountered a parable or miracle of Jesus, he took the opportunity to bring into that account any other material from the life of Messiah that was also on that particular theme.

It did not matter if the material came from a different time and place. He made clusters of material that had the same theme. For example, in Matt. 13, when Jesus introduced His first parable of the "mysteries of the kingdom of heaven," Matthew decided to throw in all other parables of the kingdom of heaven regardless of where, when, and to whom they were originally given. Matthew made clusters of the sayings and miracles of Christ as well as His parables.

Matt. 24:36-41 is a perfect example of clustering by Matthew. Neither Mark nor Luke record these words as coming out of the mouth of Jesus as He sat on Mt. Olivet. In terms of chronology, Luke records these words as being spoken by Jesus in Lk. 17:20-37. Thus they were uttered by Jesus at a different time, in a different place, and to a different audience. Matthew inserts

46

the material after v. 35 as a good time to record what Jesus said earlier about people not knowing the day or hour of His return.

The Parable of the Talents (Matt. 25:14-30) was not recorded by Mark or Luke as part of the Olivet Discourse. But in Lk. 19:11-27, Luke does record the Parable of the Pounds. It took place at a totally different place and time, with a different audience. While there are stylistic differences between these two parables, they are actually the same parable or they both came from an original parable with some minor differences.

Another indicator is found in the fact that Matthew often grouped things by three. How many parables are found in Matt. 25 that are not found in Mark or Luke? Matthew tacks on three parables at the end of the Mt. Olivet Discourse. Thus they were not originally spoken on Mt. Olivet.

Conclusion

This chapter is going to be difficult for those whose reading of Scripture is superficial at best. Most pastors have not studied the three Gospel accounts of the Discourse in parallel columns. They have not paid attention to punctuation, grammar or when Jesus goes off on tangents. They have not done their homework of studying the text with an eagle to detail. No wonder the sheep are confused when the shepherds are even more confused.

Chapter Five

The Gospel Parallel

As you read the parallel below, pay attention to the details added or omitted by each Gospel writer. It was not chance or luck that caused them to add or omit material. They chose their material carefully to stress the theme they wanted to emphasize. In order to see the entire picture of what Messiah said and did on the Mt. Olivet you must put them together side-by-side.

Matthew	Mark	Luke
24:1-2	**13:1-2**	**21:5-6**
1 Jesus came out from the temple and was going away when His disciples came up to point out the temple buildings to Him. 2 And He said to them, "Do you not see all these things? Truly I say to you, not one stone here will be left upon another, which will not be torn down."	1 As He was going out of the temple, one of His disciples said to Him, "Teacher, behold what wonderful stones and what wonderful buildings!" 2 And Jesus said to him, "Do you see these great buildings? Not one stone will be left upon another which will not be torn down."	5 And while some were talking about the temple, that it was adorned with beautiful stones and votive gifts, He said, 6 "As for these things which you are looking at, the days will come in which there will not be left one stone upon another which will not be torn down."
24:3-8	**13:3-8**	**21:7-11**
3 As He was sitting on the Mount of Olives, the disciples came to Him privately, saying, "Tell us, when will these things happen, and what will be the sign of Your coming, and of the end of the age?"	3 As He was sitting on the Mount of Olives opposite the temple, Peter and James and John and Andrew were questioning Him privately, 4 "Tell us, when will these things be, and what will be the sign when all these things	7 They questioned Him, saying, "Teacher, when therefore will these things happen? And what will be the sign when these things are about to take place?" 8 And He said, "See to it that you are not misled; for many will

49

4 And Jesus answered and said to them, "See to it that no one misleads you.	are going to be fulfilled?"	come in My name, saying, 'I am He,' and, 'The time is near 'Do not go after them.
5 "For many will come in My name, saying, 'I am the Christ,' and will mislead many.	5 And Jesus began to say to them, "See to it that no one misleads you.	
6 "You will be hearing of wars and rumors of wars. See that you are not frightened, for those things must take place, but that is not yet the end.	6 "Many will come in My name, saying, 'I am He!' and will mislead many.	9 "When you hear of wars and disturbances, do not be terrified; for these things must take place first, but the end does not follow immediately."
7 "For nation will rise against nation, and kingdom against kingdom, and in various places there will be famines and earthquakes.	7 "When you hear of wars and rumors of wars, do not be frightened; those things must take place; but that is not yet the end.	10 Then He continued by saying to them, "Nation will rise against nation and kingdom against kingdom,
8 "But all these things are merely the beginning of birth pangs.	8 "For nation will rise up against nation, and kingdom against kingdom; there will be earthquakes in various places; there will also be famines. These things are merely the beginning of birth pangs.	11 and there will be great earthquakes, and in various places plagues and famines; and there will be terrors and great signs from heaven.
24:9-14	**13:9-13**	**21:12-19**
9 "Then they will deliver you to tribulation, and will kill you, and you will be hated by all nations because of My name.	9 "But be on your guard; for they will deliver you to the courts, and you will be flogged in the synagogues, and you will stand before governors and kings for My sake, as a testimony to them.	12 "But before all these things, they will lay their hands on you and will persecute you, delivering you to the synagogues and prisons, bringing you before kings and governors for My name's sake.
10 "At that time many will fall away and will betray one another and hate one another.	10 "The gospel must first be preached to all the nations.	13 "It will lead to an opportunity for your testimony.
11 "Many false prophets will arise and will mislead many.	11 "When they arrest you and hand you	14 "So make up your minds not to prepare
12 "Because lawless-		

ness is increased, most people's love will grow cold. 13 "But the one who endures to the end, he will be saved. 14 "This gospel of the kingdom shall be preached in the whole world as a testimony to all the nations, and then the end will come.	over, do not worry beforehand about what you are to say, but say whatever is given you in that hour; for it is not you who speak, but it is the Holy Spirit. 12 "Brother will betray brother to death, and a father his child; and children will rise up against parents and have them put to death. 13 "You will be hated by all because of My name, but the one who endures to the end, he will be saved.	beforehand to defend yourselves; 15 for I will give you utterance and wisdom which none of your opponents will be able to resist or refute. 16 "But you will be betrayed even by parents and brothers and relatives and friends, and they will put some of you to death, 17 and you will be hated by all because of My name. 18 "Yet not a hair of your head will perish. 19 "By your endurance you will gain your lives.
24:15-22 15 "Therefore when you see the ABOMI-NATION OF DESO-LATION which was spoken of through Daniel the prophet, standing in the holy place (let the reader understand), 16 then those who are in Judea must flee to the mountains. 17 "Whoever is on the housetop must not go down to get the things out that are in his house. 18 "Whoever is in the field must not turn back to get his cloak. 19 "But woe to those who are pregnant and	**13:14-20** 14 "But when you see the ABOMINATION OF DESOLATION standing where it should not be (let the reader understand), then those who are in Judea must flee to the mountains. 15 "The one who is on the housetop must not go down, or go in to get anything out of his house; 16 and the one who is in the field must not turn back to get his coat. 17 "But woe to those who are pregnant and to those who are nursing babies in	**21:20-24** 20 "But when you see Jerusalem surrounded by armies, then recognize that her desolation is near. 21 "Then those who are in Judea must flee to the mountains, and those who are in the midst of the city must leave, and those who are in the country must not enter the city; 22 because these are days of vengeance, so that all things which are written will be fulfilled. 23 "Woe to those who are pregnant and to those who are nursing babies in those days;

to those who are nursing babies in those days! 20 "But pray that your flight will not be in the winter, or on a Sabbath. 21 "For then there will be a great tribulation, such as has not occurred since the beginning of the world until now, nor ever will. 22 "Unless those days had been cut short, no life would have been saved; but for the sake of the elect those days will be cut short.	those days! 18 "But pray that it may not happen in the winter. 19 "For those days will be a time of tribulation such as has not occurred since the beginning of the creation which God created until now, and never will. 20 "Unless the Lord had shortened those days, no life would have been saved; but for the sake of the elect, whom He chose, He shortened the days.	for there will be great distress upon the land and wrath to this people; 24 and they will fall by the edge of the sword, and will be led captive into all the nations; and Jerusalem will be trampled under foot by the Gentiles until the times of the Gentiles are fulfilled.
24:23-28 23 "Then if anyone says to you, 'Behold, here is the Christ,' or 'There He is,' do not believe him. 24 "For false Christs and false prophets will arise and will show great signs and wonders, so as to mislead, if possible, even the elect. 25 "Behold, I have told you in advance. 26 "So if they say to you, 'Behold, He is in the wilderness,' do not go out, or, 'Behold, He is in the inner rooms,' do not believe them. 27 "For just as the lightning comes from	**13:21-23** 21 "And then if anyone says to you, 'Behold, here is the Christ'; or, 'Behold, He is there'; do not believe him; 22 for false Christs and false prophets will arise, and will show signs and wonders, in order to lead astray, if possible, the elect. 23 "But take heed; behold, I have told you everything in advance.	**17:23-24** 23 "They will say to you, 'Look there! Look here!' Do not go away, and do not run after them. 24 "For just like the lightning, when it flashes out of one part of the sky, shines to the other part of the sky, so will the Son of Man be in His day. **17:37** 37 And answering they said to Him, "Where, Lord?" And He said to them, "Where the body is, there also the vultures will be gathered."

the east and flashes even to the west, so will the coming of the Son of Man be. 28 "Wherever the corpse is, there the vultures will gather.		
24:29-31 29 But immediately after the tribulation of those days the sun shall be darkened, and the moon shall not give her light, and the stars shall fall from heaven, and the powers of the heavens shall be shaken: 30 and then shall appear the sign of the Son of man in heaven: and then shall all the tribes of the earth mourn, and they shall see the Son of man coming on the clouds of heaven with power and great glory. 31 And he shall send forth his angels with a great sound of a trumpet, and they shall gather together his elect from the four winds, from one end of heaven to the other.	**13:24-27** 24 But in those days, after that tribulation, the sun shall be darkened, and the moon shall not give her light, 25 and the stars shall be falling from heaven, and the powers that are in the heavens shall be shaken. 26 And then shall they see the Son of man coming in clouds with great power and glory. 27 And then shall he send forth the angels, and shall gather together his elect from the four winds, from the uttermost part of the earth to the uttermost part of heaven.	**21:25-28** 25 And there shall be signs in sun and moon and stars; and upon the earth distress of nations, in perplexity for the roaring of the sea and the billows; 26 men fainting for fear, and for expectation of the things which are coming on the world: for the powers of the heavens shall be shaken. 27 And then shall they see the Son of man coming in a cloud with power and great glory. 28 But when these things begin to come to pass, look up, and lift up your heads; because your redemption draweth nigh.
24:32-41 32 "Now learn the parable from the fig tree: when its branch has already become tender and puts forth	**13:28-32** 28 "Now learn the parable from the fig tree: when its branch has already become tender and puts forth	**21:29-33** 29 Then He told them a parable: "Behold the fig tree and all the trees; 30 as soon as they

its leaves, you know that summer is near;

33 so, you too, when you see all these things, recognize that He is near, right at the door.

34 "Truly I say to you, this generation will not pass away until all these things take place.

35 "Heaven and earth will pass away, but My words will not pass away.

36 "But of that day and hour no one knows, not even the angels of heaven, nor the Son, but the Father alone.

37 "For the coming of the Son of Man will be just like the days of Noah.

38 "For as in those days before the flood they were eating and drinking, marrying and giving in marriage, until the day that Noah entered the ark,

39 and they did not understand until the flood came and took them all away; so will the coming of the Son of Man be.

40 "Then there will be two men in the field; one will be taken and one will be left.

41 "Two women will

its leaves, you know that summer is near.

29 "Even so, you too, when you see these things happening, recognize that He is near, right at the door.

30 "Truly I say to you, this generation will not pass away until all these things take place.

31 "Heaven and earth will pass away, but My words will not pass away.

32 "But of that day or hour no one knows, not even the angels in heaven, nor the Son, but the Father alone.

put forth leaves, you see it and know for yourselves that summer is now near.

31 "So you also, when you see these things happening, recognize that the kingdom of God is near.

32 "Truly I say to you, this generation will not pass away until all things take place.

33 "Heaven and earth will pass away, but My words will not pass away.

be grinding at the mill; one will be taken and one will be left.		
24:43-25:12 42 "Therefore be on the alert, for you do not know which day your Lord is coming. 43 "But be sure of this, that if the head of the house had known at what time of the night the thief was coming, he would have been on the alert and would not have allowed his house to be broken into. 44 "For this reason you also must be ready; for the Son of Man is coming at an hour when you do not think He will. 45 "Who then is the faithful and sensible slave whom his master put in charge of his household to give them their food at the proper time? 46 "Blessed is that slave whom his master finds so doing when he comes. 47 "Truly I say to you that he will put him in charge of all his possessions. 48 "But if that evil slave says in his heart, 'My master is not coming for a long time,'	**13:33-37** 33 "Take heed, keep on the alert; for you do not know when the appointed time will come. 34 "It is like a man away on a journey, who upon leaving his house and putting his slaves in charge, assigning to each one his task, also commanded the doorkeeper to stay on the alert. 35 "Therefore, be on the alert--for you do not know when the master of the house is coming, whether in the evening, at midnight, or when the rooster crows, or in the morning-- 36 in case he should come suddenly and find you asleep. 37 "What I say to you I say to all, 'Be on the alert!'"	**19:12-13** 12 So He said, "A nobleman went to a distant country to receive a kingdom for himself, and then return. 13 "And he called ten of his slaves, and gave them ten minas and said to them, 'Do business with this until I come back.' **12:40** 40 "You too, be ready; for the Son of Man is coming at an hour that you do not expect."

49 and begins to beat his fellow slaves and eat and drink with drunkards; 50 the master of that slave will come on a day when he does not expect him and at an hour which he does not know, 51 and will cut him in pieces and assign him a place with the hypocrites; in that place there will be weeping and gnashing of teeth. 1 Then the kingdom of heaven will be comparable to ten virgins, who took their lamps and went out to meet the bridegroom. 2 "Five of them were foolish, and five were prudent. 3 "For when the foolish took their lamps, they took no oil with them, 4 but the prudent took oil in flasks along with their lamps. 5 "Now while the bridegroom was delaying, they all got drowsy and began to sleep. 6 "But at midnight there was a shout, 'Behold, the bridegroom! Come out to meet him.' 7 "Then all those virgins rose and		

trimmed their lamps. 8 "The foolish said to the prudent, 'Give us some of your oil, for our lamps are going out.' 9 "But the prudent answered, 'No, there will not be enough for us and you too; go instead to the dealers and buy some for yourselves.' 10 "And while they were going away to make the purchase, the bridegroom came, and those who were ready went in with him to the wedding feast; and the door was shut. 11 "Later the other virgins also came, saying, 'Lord, lord, open up for us.' 12 "But he answered, 'Truly I say to you, I do not know you.' **25:13-15** 13 "Be on the alert then, for you do not know the day nor the hour. 14 "For it is just like a man about to go on a journey, who called his own slaves and entrusted his possessions to them. 15 "To one he gave five talents, to another, two, and to another, one, each		

according to his own ability; and he went on his journey.		
		21:34-36 34 "Be on guard, so that your hearts will not be weighted down with dissipation and drunkenness and the worries of life, and that day will not come on you suddenly like a trap; 35 for it will come upon all those who dwell on the face of all the earth. 36 "But keep on the alert at all times, praying that you may have strength to escape all these things that are about to take place, and to stand before the Son of Man."

Conclusion

No one denies that the early church clearly saw part of the Olivet discourse as relating to the destruction of Jerusalem in A.D. 70. When the Christians saw the armies of Titus approaching the city, they literally ran for the hills, as commanded by Jesus. Thus not one Christian is said to have died in the destruction of Jerusalem.

The rest of the history of the interpretation of the Olivet discourse is quite convoluted and a mass of conflicting and contradictory material. The "Babylonian Captivity" of the Church began in Alexandria, Egypt, when Greek Philosophers brought the allegorical hermeneutic into the Church and reinterpreted the Bible in ways foreign to Jews. This is why Origin's interpretation of Scripture was allegorical in nature and why he ended up teaching universalism, the pre-existence of the soul, and other pagan doctrines.

Once the Gentiles took over the Church, the knowledge of Jewish Apocalypticism disappeared from biblical interpretation. Replacement theology, dispensationalism, covenant theology, Preterism and all other Western European systems of interpretation developed in isolation from Jewish ways of interpreting the Bible. These Gentile hermeneutics should be rejected because they ignore the ethnic context and literary style of the passage. The typical Western European Gentile interpretation of the Mt. Olivet discourse is erroneous.

The Mt. Olivet Discourse should not be presented in an "either/or" dichotomy of either it was all fulfilled at A.D. 70 or none of it was fulfilled by A.D. 70. It covers events leading up the destruction of the temple and then proceeds with events leading up to the glorious return of Christ at the end of the age.

While the issue of whether the N.T. was completed before A.D. 70 is important for Preterism, in that if any references to the Second Coming of Christ or the resurrection or Judgment Day are found in a Post-70 N.T. book, Preterism is automatically false. Yet, if the N.T. was finished before A.D. 70, it does not automatically prove Preterism. A futuristic view can exist before or after A.D. 70.

As you study the Mt. Olivet Discourse as summarized by Matthew, Mark, and Luke, let this motivate you to use a Gospel harmony when studying the life and teaching of Christ. God gave us four Gospels and He expects us to compare them when possible. Don't be lazy and just rest upon one summary. "Study to show yourself approved to God" by striving for excellence in your interpretation of Scripture. Leave no stone left unturned and no evidence ignored.

PART TWO:

The Apocalypse Of Yeshua the Messiah

Introduction

The Book of Revelation (i.e. the Apocalypse) is a complete mystery to most people. It is rarely preached upon today and it seems out of place in the modern world. Yet, it has much to tell us about the past, the present, and the future.

This book is a modest introduction to the Apocalypse and is not intended to be a detailed commentary on the book. After forty years of reading and preaching on it, I am the first to admit that some of it remains a mystery to me. Yet, I have a few fresh ideas that may prove helpful to those who seek to understand the Apocalypse.

The way to profit the most from this modest work is to lay aside your preconceived ideas and dogmatic assumptions about the meaning and structure of the Apocalypse. Open your mind to fresh ideas on how to interpret the book.

To that end, we have placed a revised text of Revelation in the first chapter so that you can begin by reading through the book in one sitting. For some of you, it has been many years since you read through the Apocalypse in one sitting. Yet, there is no other way to grasp the "feel" of the book except to read it through in one sitting.

Not only would I suggest that you read the book in one sitting, but that you should also read it aloud to someone. Reading it aloud will enable you catch the pathos and feel of the book. Reading the entire book aloud at one sitting will enable you to fly over the landscape of the book and gain a perspective of the whole that only comes from such a reading.

We must also point out that the New Testament was originally written to be read out loud. There were several reasons why the Bible was written to be read out loud.

    a. The Sacred Scrolls were hand copied and were thus so expensive that the average person could not afford to own his or her own copy. This is why the scrolls were kept in the synagogue and later in the early church. Jesus went to the synagogue and asked for a copy of the Isaiah scroll so He could read it (lk. 4:16-20).

b. There are grammatical markers in the text to indicate what word should be stressed when reading it aloud. For example, the order of the words in the Greek text of John 1:1 is written to indicate to the public reader to stress the word "God" in the phrase, "and the Word was GOD!" This is one reason why the Jehovah's Witness attempt to translate it, "a god" is grammatically impossible.

c. Many of the early Christians were illiterate and who could not read Scripture even if they wanted to. They needed someone who would read it to them.

d. Faith comes from *hearing* the Word (Rom. 10:17).
There is a power in *hearing* Scripture, not just reading it silently.

e. Paul reminded Timothy not to neglect the pubic reading of Scripture (1 Tim. 4:13).

f. What a wonderful way to gather the family together for devotions. Read the entire Apocalypse to your family in one sitting.

g. Read the book with drama and voice inflection. Do not read it with a dull monotone voice. The Apocalypse is an exciting book filled with dragons, demons, battles, angels, plagues, death, destruction, striking visual images, and terrifying scenes. If you read it the way it was written to be read aloud, even your youngest children will be fascinated by it. Tolkien and Harry Potter pale in comparison to the Apocalypse.

h. Lastly, we are promised a special blessing if we read it *aloud* or hear it read. The word "read" in the Greek text of Rev. 1:3 is a word that means to read aloud. Modern translations correctly render it this way.

Chapter One

The Text of the Apocalypse

First, the seven Epistles that the aged Apostle John sent out to the seven churches selected by the risen Messiah did not have any chapter or verse divisions. While these modern divisions are helpful to enable everyone to find the same part of the text, they are notorious for being quite arbitrary and, at times, making solid exegesis difficult if not impossible. For this reason, we have removed the KJV chapter and verse divisions.

Second, the Apocalypse was written to be read *aloud*. The blessing promised is for those who read it *aloud* and for those who *hear* it.

> How blessed is the one who reads aloud and those who
> hear the words of this prophecy.

Third, the first century was a very superstitious age. The pagans believed that the world was inhabited by dragons, devils, gods, goddesses, beasts, monsters, and bizarre creatures. The recipients of the Apocalypse were Jewish Christians. While they did not believe that such creatures actually existed, the visions of John did not seem strange or bizarre to them as the beasts he described were part of the cultural context of their day. They had no problem with understanding the symbolic nature of the vivid and frightening images of heavenly and earthly battles between demons, angels, monsters, and men.

In stark contrast, today we live in a secular world where the supernatural is no longer perceived as all around us. People no longer believe in red dragons with seven heads, monstrous beasts, and devils that looked like a cross between locusts and crazy women. This is why it is a *bizarre* book to many people today!

Fourth, too often those who interpret the Apocalypse begin by imposing on it an outline that was supplied by their theological system. They assume that they already understand the Book of Revelation before reading it! This has resulted in a great deal of unnecessary controversy and dogmatism. Instead of imposing a futurist, historist, Preterist, dispensational or covenantal structure on the book, we will lay aside all preconceived Western Gentile ideas about the Apocalypse and let the book unfold itself.

Fifth, most commentators assume that the Apocalypse was outlined by John *before* he wrote it. Thus, he had a clear outline in mind when he wrote the book. But John did not write the Apocalypse in the same way that Paul wrote Romans. Instead, it was dictated word for word by the risen Messiah or by angels who spoke to John. He wrote only what he was told to write and thus he had no control of what he wrote down.

The Apocalypse is an ancient example of what we call today "stream of consciousness" writing in that John was giving a running description of the fantastic visions that came at him like freight trains. He had no control whatsoever over what he saw or heard. He described things as he experienced them.

It should thus not surprise us if we find that the Apocalypse does not have a neat and tidy structure or outline. It will jerk this way and that and violate all known literary structures.

I personally get irritated with all the neat and tidy outlines of the book that one finds in typical commentaries. They assume that John sat down and outlined his book before he wrote it. But he was minding his own business when he was suddenly kidnapped by the Holy Spirit, strapped in an apocalyptic Holy Ghost roller coaster, and taken on a wild and crazy ride.

We can only imagine the rush he got as he rode the apocalyptic roller coaster up and then down, while being jerked side to side, and could only hang on for dear life. He is on earth one moment and then in heaven and then back on earth and then taken back to heaven. He was not in control of what he saw or heard. John did not write the Apocalypse *per se*. He *experienced* it! And then he recorded his experiences.

It should thus not surprise us if we find the Apocalypse has all kinds of strange twists and turns. But this does not bother us in the least. After all, it is an "unveiling" of heavenly mysteries. It describes what human eyes have never seen (1 Cor. 2:9).

Take the time now to read it aloud to one or more people. You will be pleasantly surprised how reading it aloud enables you to sit next to John in the apocalyptic Holy Ghost roller coaster and feel the thrill and rush he felt during his visions.

Note: We have restructured the text to reflect the dynamic character original text.

The Scroll of the Apocalypse
From Messiah Jesus

Cycle One
The first Cycle introduces the author of the Apocalypse, its divine Origin, to whom it was written, the focus of the work, and the credentials of the recipient, the key word is "saw."

This is[a] the apocalypse from Messiah Jesus, which God gave him to show his servants the things that must happen soon.

He made it known by sending his angel to his servant John, who testified to **what he saw**: the word of God and the testimony about Jesus Christ.

The Promise of a special blessing to those who read or hear it and its immediate relevance.

How blessed is the one who reads aloud and those who hear the words of this prophecy and keep what is written in it, for the time is near!

The Seven Churches Chosen to Receive Letters From John

From[b] John to the seven churches in Asia.

A Salutation from the Holy Trinity.

May grace and peace be yours:
from the One who is,
who was,

---

[a] 1:1 The Gk. lacks *This is*

[b] 1:4 The Gk. lacks *From*

68

and who is coming,
from the seven spirits who are in front of his throne,
and from Jesus Christ, the witness, the faithful one,[c]
the firstborn from the dead, and the ruler over the
kings of the earth.

A Doxology to the Messiah

To the One who loves us and has freed[d] us from our sins
by his blood and has made us a kingdom, priests for his God and
Father, be glory and power forever and ever! Amen.

The First Cycle is closed with the coming of Christ at the end of
the world:

You there!
Look out!
He is coming in the clouds:
Every eye will see him,
    even those who pierced him,
        and all the tribes of the earth
will mourn because of him.

John's agreement with the End.

So be it! Amen.

God's agreement with the End.

"I am the Alpha and the Omega,"
declares the Lord God,
    the one who is,
        who was,

---

[c] 1:5 Or *Jesus Christ, the faithful witness*

[d] 1:5 Other mss. read *has washed*

and who is coming,
the Almighty.

Cycle Two

The 2nd Cycle takes place on earth and begins with a new introduction:

I am John, your brother and partner in suffering, ruling, and enduring because of Jesus. I was on the island called Patmos because of the word of God and the testimony about Jesus.

1st Audio Experience and the seven churches to which the Apocalypse was sent

I came to be in the Spirit on the Day of the Lord, when I **heard a loud voice** behind me like a trumpet, saying,

"Write on a scroll what you see, and send it to the seven churches: Ephesus, Smyrna, Pergamum, Thyatira, Sardis, Philadelphia, and Laodicea."

1st Vision in 2nd cycle: The Glorified Messiah standing among seven golden lamp stands

Then I turned to **see** the voice that was talking to me, and when I turned **I saw** seven gold lamp stands. Among the lamp stands there was someone like the Son of Man.

Seven descriptions of the glorified Messiah

He was wearing a long robe with a gold belt around his waist.

His head and his hair were white like wool, in fact, as white as snow.

His eyes were like flames of fire,

His feet were like glowing bronze refined in a furnace,

His voice was like the sound of raging waters.

In his right hand he held seven stars, and out of his mouth came a sharp, two-edged sword.

His face was like the sun when it shines with full force.

John's reaction to the vision

When I **saw** him, I fell down at his feet like a dead man.

Jesus' response to John's fainting: next audio experience

But he placed his right hand on me and said, "Stop being afraid!

Jesus declares His deity

I am the first and the last, the living one. I was dead, but look—I am alive forever and ever! I have the keys of Death and Hades.[e]

Time frame of events revealed

Therefore, write down:
what you have seen,
    what is,
and what is going to happen after this.

---

[e] 1:18 I.e. the realm of the dead

71

Explanation of symbols

The secret meaning of the seven stars that you saw in my right hand and the seven gold lamp stands is this:
the seven stars are the messengers[f] of the seven churches, and the seven lamp stands are the seven churches."

The Letter to the Church in Ephesus

"To the messenger[a] of the church in Ephesus, write:

"The One who holds the seven stars in his right hand,
the One who walks among the seven gold lamp stands, says this:
I know your works, your toil, and your endurance.
I also know that you cannot tolerate evil people.
You have tested those who call themselves apostles, but are not, and have found them to be false.
You have endured and suffered because of my name, yet you have not grown weary.
However, I have this against you: You have abandoned the love you had at first.
Therefore, remember how far you have fallen. Repent, and do the works you did at first.
If you don't, I will come to you and remove your lamp stand from its place, unless you repent.
But this is to your credit: You hate the works of the Nicolaitans, which I also hate.

Jesus' exhortation to the Ephesians to receive his letter.

---

[f] 1:20 Or *angels*

[a] 2:1 Or *angel*

'Let the person who has an ear listen to what the Spirit says to the churches. To everyone who conquers I will give the privilege of eating from the tree of life that is in the paradise of God.'"

The Letter to the Church in Smyrna

"To the messenger[b] of the church in Smyrna, write:

'The first and the last, who was dead and became alive, says this:
'I know your suffering, your poverty—though you are rich—and the slander on the part of those who claim to be Jews but aren't. They are the synagogue of Satan. Don't be afraid of what you are going to suffer. Look! The devil is going to throw some of you into prison so that you may be tested. For ten days you will undergo suffering. Be faithful until death, and I will give you the victor's crown of life.

Jesus' exhortation to the Smyrnnans to receive his letter.

'Let the person who has an ear listen to what the Spirit says to the churches. The one who conquers will never be hurt by the second death.'"

The Letter to the Church in Pergamum
"To the messenger[c] of the church in Pergamum, write:

'The one who holds the sharp, two-edged sword, says this:
'I know where you live. Satan's throne is there. Yet you hold on to my name and have not denied your faith in me,[d] even

---

[b] 2:8 Or *angel*

[c] 2:12 Or *angel*

[d] 2:13 Or *my faith*

in the days of Antipas, my faithful witness, who was killed in your presence, where Satan lives.

But I have a few things against you: You have there some who hold to the teaching of Balaam, the one who taught Balak to put a stumbling block before the people of Israel so that they would eat food sacrificed to idols and practice immorality. You also have some who hold to the teaching of the Nicolaitans. So repent. If you don't, I will come to you quickly and wage war against them with the sword of my mouth.

'Let the person who has an ear listen to what the Spirit says to the churches. To the one who conquers I will give some of the hidden manna. I will also give him a white stone. On the white stone is written a new name that no one knows except the person who receives it.'"

The Letter to the Church in Thyatira
"To the messenger[e] of the church in Thyatira, write:

'The Son of God, whose eyes are like flaming fire and whose feet are like glowing bronze, says this:'I know your works—your love, faithfulness,[f] service, and endurance— and that your last works are greater than the first.

But I have this against you: You tolerate that woman Jezebel, who calls herself a prophet and who teaches and leads my servants to practice immorality and to eat food sacrificed to idols. I gave her time to repent, but she refused to repent of her immorality.

Look! I am going to throw her into a sickbed. Those who commit adultery with her will also have great suffering, unless they repent of her works. I will strike her children dead. Then all the churches will know that I am the one who searches minds and hearts. I will reward each of you as your works deserve.

---

[e] 2:18 Or *angel*

[f] 2:19 Or *faith*

'But as for the rest of you in Thyatira—you who do not hold on to this teaching and who have not learned what some people call the deep things of Satan—I won't lay on you any other burden. Just hold on to what you have until I come.

To the person who conquers and continues to do my works to the end I will give authority over the nations. He will rule them with an iron scepter, as when clay pots are shattered. Just as I have received authority from my Father, I will also give him the morning star.

Jesus' exhortation to the Thyatirans to receive his letter.

'Let the person who has an ear listen to what the Spirit says to the churches.'"
The Letter to the Church in Sardis
"To the messenger[a] of the church in Sardis, write:

'The one who has the seven spirits of God and the seven stars says this:
'I know your works. You are known for being alive, but you are dead. Be alert, and strengthen the things that are left, which are about to die. I have not found your works to be completed in the sight of my God. So remember what you received and heard. Obey it, and repent. If you are not alert, I will come like a thief, and you won't know the time when I will come to you. But you have a few people in Sardis who have not soiled their clothes. They will walk with me in white clothes because they are worthy. The person who conquers in this way will wear white clothes, and I will never erase his name from the Book of Life. I will acknowledge his name in the presence of my Father and his angels.

Jesus' exhortation to the Sardists to receive his letter.

---

[a] 3:1 Or *angel*

'Let the person who has an ear listen to what the Spirit says to the churches.'"

The Letter to the Church in Philadelphia

"To the messenger[b] of the church in Philadelphia, write:
'The one who is holy, who is true,

who has the key of David,

who opens

a door that[c] no one can shut,

and who shuts a door that[d] no one can open,

says this:

I know your works. Look! I have put in front of you an open door that no one can shut. You have only a little strength, but you have kept my word and have not denied my name. I will make those who belong to the synagogue of Satan—those who claim to be Jews and aren't, but are lying—come and bow down at your feet. Then they will realize that I have loved you. Because you have kept my command to endure,[e] I will keep you from the hour of testing that is coming to the whole world to test those living on the earth.

I am coming soon! Hold on to what you have so that no one takes your victor's crown.

I will make the one who conquers a pillar in the sanctuary of my God, and he will never go out of it again. I will write on him the name of my God, the name of the city of my

---

[b] 3:7 Or *angel*

[c] 3:7 Lit. *who opens and*

[d] 3:7 Lit. *who shuts and*

[e] 3:10 Lit. *my word of endurance*

God (the new Jerusalem coming down out of heaven from God), and my own new name.

Jesus' exhortation to the Philadelphians to receive His letter.

"Let the person who has an ear listen to what the Spirit says to the churches."

The Letter to the Church in Laodicea

"To the messenger[f] of the church in Laodicea, write:

'The Amen, the witness who is faithful and true, the beginning[g] of God's creation, says this:
'I know your works, that you are neither cold nor hot. I wish you were cold or hot.
Since you are lukewarm and neither hot nor cold, I am going to spit you out of my mouth.
You say, "I am rich. I have become wealthy. I don't need anything." Yet you don't realize that you are miserable, pitiful, poor, blind, and naked.
Therefore, I advise you to buy from me gold purified in fire so that you may be rich, white clothes to wear so that you may keep the shame of your nakedness from showing, and ointment to put on your eyes so that you may see. I correct and discipline those whom I love, so be serious and repent!
Look! I am standing at the door and knocking. If anyone listens to my voice and opens the door, I will come in to him and eat with him, and he will eat[h] with me.

---

[f] 3:14 Or *angel*

[g] 3:14 Or *source*

[h] 3:20 The Gk. lacks *will eat*

To the one who conquers I will give a place to sit with me on my throne, just as I have conquered and have sat down with my Father on his throne.

Admonition to the Laodiceans to receive his letter.

'Let the person who has an ear listen to what the Spirit says to the churches.'"

End of Second Cycle.

Cycle Three: visions seen in heaven.

1st Vision in 3rd Cycle:

After these things I **saw** a door standing open in heaven.

Audio experience:

The first voice, which I had **heard** speaking to me like a trumpet, said,

"Come up here, and I will show you what must happen after this."

2nd Vision in 3rd Cycle. John is transported from earth to heaven.

Instantly I was in the Spirit, and **I saw** a throne in heaven with a person seated on the throne. The person sitting there looked like jasper and carnelian, and there was a rainbow around the throne that looked like an emerald.

Around the throne were twenty-four other thrones, and on these thrones sat twenty-four elders wearing white robes and gold victor's crowns on their heads. Flashes of lightning, noises, and peals of thunder came from the throne. Burning in front of the throne were seven flaming torches, which are the seven spirits of God.

In front of the throne was something like a sea of glass as clear as crystal. In the center of the throne and on each side of the throne were four living creatures full of eyes in front and in back.

The first living creature was like a lion, the second living creature was like an ox, the third living creature had a face like a human, and the fourth living creature was like a flying eagle. Each of the four living creatures had six wings and were full of eyes inside and out. Without stopping day or night they were saying,

> "Holy, holy, holy
> is the Lord God Almighty,
> who was, who is, and who is coming."

Whenever the living creatures give glory, honor, and thanks to the one who sits on the throne, who lives forever and ever, the twenty-four elders bow down in front of the one who sits on the throne and worship the one who lives forever and ever. They throw their victor's crowns in front of the throne and say,

A hymn to the Father

> "You are worthy, our Lord and God,
> to receive glory, honor, and power,
> because you created all things,
> and they came into existence
> and were created because of your will."

3rd Vision in 3rd Cycle: the Scroll with Seven Seals

Then **I saw** in the right hand of the one who sits on the throne a scroll written on the inside and on the outside, sealed with seven seals.

4th Vision in 3rd Cycle: The Angel's announcement

I **also saw** a powerful angel proclaiming with a loud voice,

"Who is worthy to open the scroll and break its seals?"

No one in heaven, on earth, or under the earth could open the scroll or look inside it.

I began to cry bitterly because no one was found worthy to open the scroll or look inside it. Then one of the elders said to me, "Stop crying. Look! The Lion from the tribe of Judah, the Root of David, has conquered. He can open the scroll and its seven seals."

[5th] Vision in [3rd] Cycle: the Lamb Takes the Scroll

Then **I saw** a lamb standing in the middle of the throne, the four living creatures, and the elders. He looked[a] like he had been slaughtered. He had seven horns and seven eyes, which are the seven spirits of God sent into all the earth. He went and took the scroll from the right hand of the one who sits on the throne.

When the lamb had taken the scroll, the four living creatures and the twenty-four elders bowed down in front of him. Each held a harp and a gold bowl full of incense, the prayers of the saints. They sang a new song:

A heavenly hymn to the Son

> "You are worthy to take the scroll and open its seals, because you were slaughtered. With your blood you purchased people[b] for God from every tribe, language, people, and nation. You made them a kingdom and priests for our God, and they will reign on the earth."

---

[a] 5:6 The Gk. lacks *He looked*

[b] 5:9 The Gk. lacks *people*

6th Vision in 3rd Cycle and next audio experience: the worship of the Lamb

Then I **looked**, and I **heard** the voices of many angels, the living creatures, and the elders surrounding the throne. They numbered 10,000 times 10,000 and thousands times thousands.

A heavenly hymn to the Son

They sang with a loud voice,

"Worthy is the lamb who was slaughtered to receive power, wealth, wisdom, strength, honor, glory, and praise!"

Audio experience: A universal Doxology to the Father and the Son

I **heard** every creature in heaven, on earth, under the earth, and on the sea, and everything that is in them, saying,

"To the one who sits on the throne and to the lamb be praise, honor, glory, and power forever and ever!"

Then the four living creatures said, "Amen!", and the elders bowed down and worshiped.

7th Vision in 3rd Cycle: the First Seal Opened

Then I **saw** the lamb open the first of the seven seals.

Audio experience:

I **heard** one of the four living creatures say with a voice like thunder, "Go!"

8th Vision in 3rd Cycle: The white horse

Then I **looked**, and there was a white horse! Its rider had a bow, and a victor's crown had been given to him. He went out as a conqueror to conquer.

9th Vision in 3rd Cycle : the Second Seal Opened

[Then I saw] the lamb[a] open the second seal.

Audio Experience:

Then I **heard** the second living creature say, "Go!"

10th Vision in 3rd Cycle: the red horse

A second horse went out. It was fiery red, and its rider was given permission to take peace away from the earth and to make people slaughter one another. So he was given a large sword.

11th Vision in 3rd Cycle: the Third Seal Opened

Then I saw lamb[b] open the third seal.

Audio Experience:

Then I heard the third living creature say, "Go!"

---

[a] 6:3 Lit. *he*

[b] 6:5 Lit. *he*

12th Vision in 3rd Cycle: the black horse

I **looked,** and there was a black horse! Its rider held a scale in his hand.

Audio experience:

I **heard** what sounded like a voice from among the four living creatures, saying,

"A quart of wheat for a denarius, or three quarts of barley for a denarius.[c] But don't damage the olive oil or the wine!"

13th Vision in 3rd Cycle: the Fourth Seal Opened

Then I saw the lamb[d] open the fourth seal.

Audio experience:

I **heard** the voice of the fourth living creature say, "Go!"

14th Vision in 3rd Cycle: the pale horse

Then I **looked,** and there was a pale horse! Its rider's name was Death, and Hades[e] followed him. They were given authority over one-fourth of the earth to kill people using wars, famines, plagues, and the wild animals of the earth.

15th Vision in 3rd Cycle: the Fifth Seal Opened

---

[c] 6:6 A denarius was equivalent to a day's wage for a laborer.

[d] 6:7 Lit. *he*

[e] 6:8 I.e. the realm of the dead

When the lamb[f] opened the fifth seal. **I saw** under the altar the souls of those who had been slaughtered because of the word of God and the testimony they had given.

Audio experience:
They cried out in a loud voice,

"Holy and true Sovereign, how long will it be before you judge and take revenge on those living on the earth who shed our blood?"

16th Vision in 3rd Cycle:

[Then I saw] each of them was given a white robe. They were told to rest a little longer until the number of their fellow servants and their brothers was completed, who would be killed as they had been killed.

17th Vision in 3rd Cycle: the Sixth Seal Opened

Then **I saw** the lamb[g] open the sixth seal.
There was a powerful earthquake.
The sun turned as black as sackcloth made of hair, and the full moon turned as red as blood.[h]
The stars in the sky fell to the earth like a fig tree drops its fruit when it is shaken by a strong wind. The sky vanished like a scroll being rolled up, and every mountain and island was moved from its place.

18th Vision in 3rd Cycle: The Day of Judgment arrives and closes Cycle 3.

---

[f] 6:9 Lit. *he*

[g] 6:12 Lit. *him*

[h] 6:12 Lit. *became like blood*

Then [I saw] the kings of the earth, the important people, the generals, the rich, the powerful, and all the slaves and free people hid themselves in caves and among the rocks in the mountains.

Audio experience:

They said to the mountains and rocks,

"Fall on us and hide us from the face of the one who sits on the throne and from the wrath of the lamb. For the great Day of their wrath has come, and who is able to endure it?"

The End of the world once again described.

Cycle Four

1st Vision in 4th Cycle: four angels, four corners, and four winds
After this **I saw** four angels standing at the four corners of the earth.
They were holding back the four winds of the earth so that no wind could blow on the land, on the sea, or on any tree.

2nd Vision in 4th Cycle: A fifth angel

I **saw** another angel coming from the east having the seal of the living God. He cried out in a loud voice to the four angels who had been permitted to harm the land and sea,
"Don't harm the land, the sea, or the trees until we have marked the servants of our God with a seal on their foreheads."

Audio experience: The 144,000 introduced

I **heard** the number of those who were sealed: 144,000. Those who were sealed were from every tribe of Israel:
12,000 from the tribe of Judah were sealed,
12,000 from the tribe of Reuben,

12,000 from the tribe of Gad,
12,000 from the tribe of Asher,
12,000 from the tribe of Naphtali,
12,000 from the tribe of Manasseh,
12,000 from the tribe of Simeon,
12,000 from the tribe of Levi,
12,000 from the tribe of Issachar,
12,000 from the tribe of Zebulun,
12,000 from the tribe of Joseph,
and 12,000 from the tribe of Benjamin were sealed.

3rdth Vision in 4th Cycle: The Numberless Crowd

After this, **I looked again**, and there was a large crowd that no one was able to count! They were from every nation, tribe, people, and language. They were standing in front of the throne and the lamb and were wearing white robes, with palm branches in their hands.

Audio experience: A doxology to the Father and the Son

They cried out in a loud voice,

"Salvation belongs to our God,
who sits on the throne, and to the lamb!"

4th Vision in 4th Cycle:

Then I saw all the angels who stood around the throne and around the elders and the four living creatures. They fell on their faces in front of the throne and worshiped God,

Audio experience: A doxology to the Father saying,

"Amen! Praise, glory, wisdom, thanks, honor, power, and strength be to our God forever and ever! Amen!"

Audio experience: Explanation of symbol

5th Vision in 4th Cycle: The Paradise that awaits the righteous after the End.

Then [I saw] one of the elders and he said to me,

"Who are these people wearing white robes, and where did they come from?"

I said to him,
"Sir, you know."

Then he told me,

"These are the people who are coming out of the terrible suffering.[a] They have washed their robes and made them white in the blood of the lamb. [15]That is why:

"They are in front of the throne of God and worship[b] him night and day in his temple. The one who sits on the throne will shelter them. They will never be hungry or thirsty again. Neither the sun nor any burning heat will ever strike them, for the lamb in the center of the throne will be their shepherd. He will lead them to springs filled with the water of life, and God will wipe every tear from their eyes."[c]

6st Vision in 4th Cycle: the Seventh Seal Opened

When the lamb[a] opened the seventh seal, there was silence in heaven for about half an hour.

---

[a] 7:14 Or *great tribulation*

[b] 7:15 Or *serve*

[c] 7:17 Isa 25:8

[a] 8:1 Lit. *he*

7th Vision in 4th Cycle: Seven Angels Given Seven Trumpets

Then I **saw** the seven angels who stand in God's presence, and seven trumpets were given to them.

8th Vision in 4th Cycle: A fifth angel with a golden censer

Then I saw another angel came with a gold censer and stood at the altar. He was given a large quantity of incense to offer on the gold altar before the throne, along with the prayers of all the saints.

Explanation of symbols:

The smoke from the incense and the prayers of the saints went up from the angel's hand to God.

9th Vision in 4th Cycle:

The angel took the censer, filled it with fire from the altar, and threw it on the earth. Then there were peals of thunder, noises, flashes of lightning, and an earthquake.

10th Vision in 4th Cycle:

Then I saw the seven angels who had the seven trumpets got ready to blow them.

11th Vision in 4th Cycle: the First Four Trumpets

Then I saw when the first angel blew his trumpet, hail and fire were mixed with blood and thrown on the earth. One-third of the earth was burned up, one-third of the trees was burned up, and all the green grass was burned up.

When the second angel blew his trumpet, something like a huge mountain burning with fire was thrown into the sea. One-third of the sea turned into blood, one-third of the creatures that were living in the sea died, and one-third of the ships was destroyed.

When the third angel blew his trumpet, a huge star blazing like a torch fell from heaven. It fell on one-third of the rivers and on the springs of water. The name of the star is Wormwood. One-third of the water turned into wormwood, and many people died from the water because it had turned bitter.

When the fourth angel blew his trumpet, one-third of the sun, one-third of the moon, and one-third of the stars were struck so that one-third of them turned dark. One-third of the day was kept from shining, and also the night.

12th Vision in 4th Cycle: the flying Eagle and new audio experience interrupts cycle of trumpets.

Then I **looked**, and I **heard** an eagle flying overhead say in a loud voice,

"How terrible, how terrible, how terrible for those living on the earth, because of the blasts of the remaining trumpets that the three angels are about to blow!"

13th Vision in 4th Cycle: the fifth trumpet, a falling star, a key, the bottomless pit, locust demons, Apollyon.

When the fifth angel blew his trumpet, **I saw** a star that had fallen to earth from the sky.[a]

The star[b] was given the key to the shaft of the bottomless pit.

It opened the shaft of the bottomless pit, and smoke came out of the shaft like the smoke from a large furnace.

The sun and the air were darkened with the smoke from the shaft.

Locusts came out of the smoke onto the earth, and they were given power like the power of earthly scorpions. They were told not to harm the grass on the earth, any green plant, or any tree. They could harm[c] only the people who do not have the seal of God on their foreheads. They were not allowed to kill them, but were only allowed[d] to torture them for five months.

Their torture was like the pain of a scorpion when it stings someone. In those days people will look for death and never find it. They will long to die, but death will escape them.

The locusts looked like horses prepared for battle. On their heads were victor's crowns that looked like gold, and their faces were like human faces. They had hair like women's hair and teeth like lions' teeth. They had breastplates like iron, and the noise of their wings was like the roar of chariots with many horses rushing into battle. They had tails and stingers like scorpions, and they had the power to hurt people with their tails for five months.

They had the angel of the bottomless pit ruling over them as king. In Hebrew he is called Abaddon,[e] and in Greek he is called Apollyon.[f]

---

[a] 9:1 Or *from heaven*

[b] 9:1 Lit. *It*

[c] 9:4 The Gk. lacks *They could harm*

[d] 9:5 The Gk. lacks *were only allowed*

[e] 9:11 I.e. the realm of destruction in the afterlife

[f] 9:11 I.e. Destroyer

The first catastrophe is over.

After these things there are still two more catastrophes to come.

14th Vision in 4th Cycle: the Sixth Trumpet, the four angels

When [I saw] the sixth angel blew his trumpet,

Audio experience

I **heard** a voice from the four[g] horns of the gold altar in front of God. It said to the sixth angel, who had the trumpet,

"Release the four angels who are held at the great Euphrates River."

So the four angels who were ready for that hour, day, month, and year were released to kill one-third of humanity. The number of cavalry troops was 200,000,000. **I heard** how many there were.[h]

15th Vision in 4th Cycle: the horse symbols described

This was how **I saw** the horses in my vision:

The riders wore breastplates that had the color of fire, sapphire, and sulfur.

The heads of the horses were like lions' heads, and fire, smoke, and sulfur came out of their mouths.

Explanation of symbols:

---

[g] 9:13 Other mss. lack *four*

[h] 9:16 Lit. *heard their number*

By these three plagues: the fire, the smoke, and the sulfur that came out of their mouths, one-third of humanity was killed.

For the power of these horses is in their mouths and their tails.

Their tails have heads like snakes, which they use to inflict pain.

The rest of the people who survived these plagues did not repent of the works of their hands or stop worshiping demons and idols made of gold, silver, bronze, stone, and wood, which cannot see, hear, or walk.

They did not repent of their murders, their deeds of witchcraft, their acts of sexual immorality, or their thefts.

16th Vision in 4th Cycle: another Powerful Angel, seven thunders, the small scroll

Then **I saw** another powerful angel come down from heaven.
He was dressed in a cloud,
and there was a rainbow over his head.
His face was like the sun,
and his legs were like columns of fire.
He held a small, opened scroll in his hand.

Setting his right foot on the sea and his left foot on the land, he shouted in a loud voice as a lion roars.

When he shouted, the seven thunders spoke with voices of their own.

Audio Experience:

When the seven thunders spoke, I was going to write, but **I heard** a voice from heaven say,

"Seal up what the seven thunders have said, and don't write it down."

17th Vision in 4th Cycle: The angel makes a vow

Then the angel whom I saw standing on the sea and on the land raised his right hand to heaven.

He swore an oath by the one who lives forever and ever, who created heaven and everything in it, the earth and everything in it, and the sea and everything in it:

"There will be no more delay. In the days when the seventh angel is ready to blow his trumpet, the secret of God will be fulfilled, as he had announced to his servants, the prophets." Audio Experience:

Then the voice that I had **heard** from heaven spoke to me again, saying,

"Go and take the opened scroll from the hand of the angel who is standing on the sea and on the land."

So I went to the angel and asked him to give me the small scroll. He said to me,

"Take it and eat it. It will be bitter in your stomach, but it will be as sweet as honey in your mouth."

So I took the small scroll from the angel's hand and ate it. It was as sweet as honey in my mouth, but when I had eaten it, my stomach was bitter.

Then the seven thunders[a] told me,

---

[a] 10:11 Lit. *they*

"Again you must prophesy about many peoples, nations, languages, and kings."

18th Vision in 4th Cycle: the stick, the temple, the two witnesses, the beast

Then I was given a stick like a measuring rod. I was told,

"Stand up and measure the temple of God and the altar, and count[a] those who worship there. But don't measure the courtyard outside the temple. Leave that out, because it is given to the nations, and they will trample the Holy City[b] for 40-two months. I will give my two witnesses who wear sackcloth the authority to prophesy for 1,260 days."

Explanation of Symbols

"These witnesses[c] are the two olive trees and the two lamp stands standing in the presence of the Lord of the earth. And if anyone should want to hurt them, fire comes out of their mouths and burns up their enemies. If anyone wants to hurt them, he must be killed in the same way.
These witnesses[d] have authority to shut the sky in order to keep rain from falling during the days of their prophesying. They also have authority over the waters to turn them into blood and to strike the earth with any plague as often as they desire.
When they have finished their testimony, the beast that comes up from the bottomless pit will wage war against them, conquer them, and kill them.

---

[a] 11:1 The Gk. lacks *count*

[b] 11:2 I.e. Jerusalem

[c] 11:4 Lit. *These ones*

[d] 11:6 Lit. *They*

Their dead bodies will lie in the street of the great city that is spiritually called Sodom and Egypt, where their Lord was crucified.

For three and a half days some members of the peoples, tribes, languages, and nations will look at their dead bodies and will not allow them to be placed in a tomb.

Those living on earth will gloat over them, celebrate, and send gifts to each other, because these two prophets had tormented those living on earth.

But after the three and a half days, the breath of life from God entered them, and they stood on their feet. Those who watched them were terrified.

Then the witnesses[e] heard a loud voice from heaven calling to them, "Come up here!"

So they went up to heaven in a cloud, and their enemies watched them.

At that moment a powerful earthquake struck.

One-tenth of the city collapsed, 7,000 people were killed by the earthquake, and the rest were terrified and gave glory to the God of heaven.

The second catastrophe is over. The third catastrophe is coming very soon.

19th Vision in 4th Cycle: the Seventh Angel Blows His Trumpet and the End of the world takes place again

When the seventh angel blew his trumpet, there were loud voices in heaven, saying,

"The kingdom of the world has become the kingdom of our Lord and of his Christ,[f] and he will rule forever and ever."

---

[e] 11:12 Lit. *they*; other mss. read *I*

[f] 11:15 I.e. Messiah

The Day of Judgment takes place and Cycle 4 comes to a close.

Then the twenty-four elders who were sitting on their thrones in God's presence fell on their faces and worshiped God. They said,
"We give thanks to you, Lord God Almighty, who is and who was, because you have taken your great power and have begun to rule. The nations were angry, but your wrath has come. It is time for the dead to be judged—to reward your servants, the prophets, the saints, and all who fear your name, both unimportant and important, and to destroy those who destroy the earth."

Cycle Five

1st Vision of 5th Cycle: the temple opened

Then [I saw] the temple of God in heaven was opened, and the ark of his covenant was seen inside his temple. There were flashes of lightning, noises, peals of thunder, an earthquake, and heavy hail.

2nd Vision of 5th Cycle: A Woman Dressed with the Sun with the moon under her feet

And I saw a spectacular sign appeared in the sky: a woman dressed with the sun, who had the moon under her feet and a victor's crown of twelve stars on her head. She was pregnant and was crying out from labor pains and the agony of giving birth.

3rd Vision of 5th Cycle: the Red Dragon

And I saw then another sign appeared in the sky:

A huge red dragon with seven heads, ten horns, and seven royal crowns on its heads.

Its tail swept away one-third of the stars in the sky and threw them down to the earth.

Then the dragon stood in front of the woman who was about to give birth so that it could devour her child when it was born.

She gave birth to a son, a boy, who is to rule[a] all the nations with an iron scepter. But her child was snatched away and taken to God and to his throne. Then the woman fled into the wilderness, where a place had been prepared for her by God so that she might be taken care of for 1,260 days.

4th Vision of 5th Cycle: a War in Heaven breaks out

And then I **saw** a war broke out in heaven:
Michael and his angels fought with the dragon, and the dragon and its angels fought back. But it was not strong enough, and there was no longer any place for them in heaven.
The huge dragon was thrown down.

Explanation of symbols:

That ancient serpent, called devil and Satan, the deceiver of the whole world, was thrown down to the earth, and its angels were thrown down with it.

Cycle Five closes with the announcement that the End has come and the kingdom of Messiah has now been set up

Then I **heard** a loud voice in heaven say,

---

[a] 12:5 Or *shepherd*

"Now the salvation, the power, he kingdom of our God, and the authority of his Christ[b] have come. For the one accusing our brothers, the one who accuses them day and night in the presence of our God, has been thrown out. They conquered him by the blood of the lamb and by the word of their testimony, for they did not love their life even in the face of death.

So be glad, heavens, and those who live in them! How terrible it is for the earth   and the sea, because the devil has come down to you with great wrath, knowing that his time is short!"

Cycle Six

1st Vision of 6th Cycle: the Dragon persecutes the Woman and Her Children

And then I saw when the dragon saw that it had been thrown down to the earth, it persecuted[c] the woman who had given birth to the boy.

However, the woman was given the two wings of a large eagle so that she could fly away from the serpent to her place in the wilderness, where she could be taken care of for a time, times, and half a time.

From its mouth the serpent poured water like a river behind the woman in order to sweep her away with the flood.

But the earth helped the woman by opening its mouth and swallowing the river that the dragon had poured from its mouth.

Then the dragon became angry with the woman and went away to do battle against the rest of her children, the ones who

---

[b] 12:10 I.e. Messiah

[c] 12:13 Or *pursued*

keep God's commandments and hold on to the testimony about Jesus. Then the dragon[d] stood on the sand of the seashore.

2nd Vision of 6th Cycle: the Beast from the Sea

Then I **saw** a beast coming out of the sea. It had ten horns, seven heads, and ten royal crowns on its horns. On its heads were blasphemous names. The beast that I saw was like a leopard. Its feet were like bear's feet, and its mouth was like a lion's mouth. The dragon gave it his power, his throne, and complete authority.

One of the beast's[a] heads looked like it had a fatal wound, but its fatal wound was healed. And in amazement the whole world followed the beast. They worshiped the dragon because it had given authority to the beast. They also worshiped the beast, saying,

"Who is like the beast, and who can fight a war with it?"

The beast was allowed[b] to speak arrogant and blasphemous things, and it was given authority for 40-two months.

It opened its mouth to utter blasphemies against God and to blaspheme his name and his residence,[c] that is, those who are living in heaven. It was allowed to wage war against the saints and to conquer them.[d]

It was also given authority over every tribe, people, language, and nation.

All those living on earth will worship it, everyone whose name is not written in the Book of Life belonging to the lamb that was slaughtered from the foundation of the world.

---

[d] 12:18 Lit. *it*; other mss. read *I*

[a] 13:3 Lit. *its*

[b] 13:5 Lit. *was given a mouth*

[c] 13:6 Lit. *tent*

[d] 13:7 Other mss. lack *It was allowed to wage war against the saints and to conquer them.*

Exhortation to readers:

Let anyone who has an ear listen:

"If anyone is to be taken captive, he must go into captivity. If anyone is to be killed with a sword, he must be killed with a sword. This is what the endurance and faith of the saints means."

3rd Vision of 6th Cycle: Another Beast appears
Then **I saw** another beast coming up out of the earth.

Seven descriptions of the Beast

It had two horns like a lamb

and it talked like a dragon.

It uses all the authority of the first beast on its behalf,[e]

and it makes the earth and those living on it worship the first beast, whose fatal wound was healed.

It performs spectacular signs, even making fire come down from heaven to earth in front of people.

It deceives those living on earth with the signs that it is allowed to do on behalf of[f] the first[g] beast, telling them to make an image for the beast who was wounded by a sword and yet lived.

4th Vision of 6th Cycle: The powers of the 2nd beast

---

[e] 13:12 Or *in its presence*

[f] 13:14 Or *in the presence of*

[g] 13:14 The Gk. lacks *first*

The second beast[h] was allowed to give breath to the image of the first[i] beast so that the image of the beast could talk and put to death those who would not worship the image of the beast.

The second beast[j] forces all people—important and unimportant, rich and poor, free and slaves—to be marked on their right hands or on their foreheads, so that no one may buy or sell unless he has the mark, which is the beast's name or the number of its name.

Explanation of symbols

This calls for wisdom:

Let the person who has understanding figure out the number of the beast, because it is the number of a person.[k] Its number is 666.[l]

5th Vision of 6th Cycle: the Lamb and the 144,000 on Mount Zion

Then **I looked**, and there was the lamb standing on Mount Zion!

With him were 144,000 people who had his name and his Father's name written on their foreheads.

Audio Experience: A New Song

---

[h] 13:15 Lit. *It*

[i] 13:15 The Gk. lacks *first*

[j] 13:16 Lit. *It*

[k] 13:18 Or *it is a human number*

[l] 13:18 Other mss. read *616*

Then **I heard** a voice from heaven like the sound of many waters and like the sound of loud thunder. The voice I **heard** was like the sound of harpists playing on their harps.

They were singing a new song in front of the throne, the four living creatures, and the elders.

No one could learn the song except the 144,000 who had been redeemed from the earth.

They have not defiled themselves with women, for they are virgins, and they follow the lamb wherever he goes.

They have been redeemed from among humanity as the first fruits for God and the lamb. In their mouth no lie was found. They are blameless.

6th Vision of 6th Cycle: the first angel preaches the eternal gospel and announces the Hour of Judgment has come

Then **I saw** another angel flying overhead with the eternal gospel to proclaim to those who live[a] on earth—to every nation, tribe, language, and people. He said in a loud voice,

"Fear God and give him glory, because the **hour of His judgment has come.** Worship the One who made heaven and earth, the sea and springs of water."

7th Vision of 6th Cycle: A second angel announces the End time judgment of Babylon the Great

[And then I saw] another angel, a second one, followed him, saying,

"Fallen! Babylon the Great **has fallen**! She has made all the nations drink the wine of the wrath of her sexual sins."

8th Vision of 6th Cycle: A third angel announces the End has come.

---

[a] 14:6 Lit. *sit*

Then [I saw] another angel, a third one, followed them, saying in a loud voice,

"Whoever worships the beast and its image and receives a mark on his forehead or his hand will drink the wine of God's wrath, which has been poured unmixed into the cup of his anger. He will be tortured with fire and sulfur in the presence of the holy angels and the lamb. The smoke from their torture goes up forever and ever. There is no rest day or night for those who worship the beast and its image or for anyone who receives the mark of its name."

A Call for Endurance

Here is a call for[b] the endurance of the saints, who keep the commandments of God and hold on to the faithfulness of Jesus.[c]

Audio Experience:

Then I **heard** a voice from heaven say,

"Write this: How blessed are the dead who die in the Lord from now on!"   "Yes," says the Spirit. "Let them rest from their labors, for their deeds follow them."

9th Vision of 6th Cycle: the white cloud and the Son of man

---

[b] 14:12 The Gk. lacks *a call for*

[c] 14:12 Or *to their faithfulness in Jesus*

Then I **looked**, and there was a white cloud! On the cloud sat someone who was like the Son of Man, with a gold victor's crown on his head and a sharp sickle in his hand.

10th Vision of 6th Cycle: The fourth angel from the temple

[Then I saw] another angel came out of the temple, crying out in a loud voice to the one who sat on the cloud,

"Swing your sickle, and gather the harvest, for the hour has come to gather it, because the harvest on the earth is fully ripe."

11th Vision of 6th Cycle: The earth harvested

[Then I saw] the one who sat on the cloud swung his sickle over the earth, and the earth was harvested.

12th Vision of 6th Cycle: Another angel with a sickle.

Then [I saw] another angel came out of the temple in heaven. He, too, had a sharp sickle.

13th Vision of 6th Cycle: a sixth angel speaks to the fifth angel

[And I saw] from the altar came another angel who had authority over fire. He called out in a loud voice to the [fifth] angel[d] who had the sharp sickle,

"Swing your sharp sickle, and gather the bunches of grapes from the vine of the earth, because those grapes are ripe."

---

[d] 14:18 Lit. *to the one*

14th Vision of 6th Cycle: The fifth angel swings his sickle and throws the enemies of God into the wrath of God.

So the [fifth] angel swung his sickle on the earth and gathered the grapes from the earth and **threw them into the great winepress of God's wrath.**

The wine press was trampled outside the city, and blood flowed out of the wine press as high as a horse's bridle for about 183 miles.[e]

15th Vision of 6th Cycle: Seven Angels with Seven Plagues bring about the wrath of God to completion.
   I saw another sign in heaven.
   It was spectacular and amazing.
   There were seven angels with the seven last plagues.
   With them God's wrath has come to its completion.

With the judgment completed, Cycle 6 closes and Cycle 7 begins.

Cycle Seven

1 st Vision of Cycle 7: the Sea of Glass

   Then **I saw** what looked like a sea of glass mixed with fire.
   Those who had conquered the beast, its image, and the number of its name were standing on the sea of glass holding God's harps in their hands. They sang the song of God's servant Moses and the song of the lamb:

   "Your deeds are spectacular and amazing, Lord God Almighty.

---

[e] 14:20 Lit. *1,600 stadia*; The Roman mile contained eight stadia, one stadion was about 604.5 feet long.

Your ways are just and true, King of the nations.[a]
Lord, who won't fear and praise your name?
For you alone are holy, and all the nations will come and worship you because your judgments have been revealed."

2 nd Vision in Cycle 7: the Temple Opened and seven angels with seven pladgues.

After these things **I looked**, and the temple of the tent of witness in heaven was open!

The seven angels with the seven plagues came out of the temple wearing clean, shininglinen with gold belts around their waists.

One of the four living creatures gave to the seven angels seven gold bowls full of the wrath of God, who lives forever and ever.

The temple was filled with smoke from the glory of God and his power, and no one could enter the temple until the seven plagues of the seven angels came to an end.

Audio Experience

Then **I heard** a loud voice from the temple saying to the seven angels,

"Go and pour the seven bowls of God's wrath on the earth."

3rd Vision in Cycle 7: the first angel with the first bowl

So [I saw] the first angel went and poured his bowl on the earth. A horrible, painful sore appeared on the people who had the mark of the beast and worshiped the image.

4th Vision in Cycle 7: the second angel with the second bowl

---

[a] 15:3 Other mss. read *of the ages*

[I saw] the second angel pour his bowl into the sea. It became like the blood of a dead body, and every living thing in the sea died.

5th Vision in Cycle 7: the third angel with the third bowl

[I saw] the third angel pour his bowl into the rivers and the springs of water, and they turned into blood.

Audio Experience

Then **I heard** the angel of the water say,

"You are just. You are the one who is and who was, the Holy One, because you have judged these things. You have given them blood to drink because they have poured out the blood of saints and prophets. This is what they deserve."

Audio Experience

[7]Then **I heard** the altar reply,

"Yes, Lord God Almighty, your judgments are true and just."

6th Vision in Cycle 7: the fourth angel with the fourth bowl

[I saw] the fourth angel pour his bowl on the sun. It was allowed to burn people with fire, and they were burned by the fierce heat. They cursed the name of God, who has the authority over these plagues. They did not repent and give him glory.

7th Vision in Cycle 7: the fifth angel with the fifth bowl

[Then I saw] the fifth angel pour his bowl on the throne of the beast. Its kingdom was plunged into darkness. People[a] gnawed on their tongues in anguish and cursed the God of heaven because of their pains and sores. But they did not repent of their deeds.

8th Vision in Cycle 7: the sixth angel with the sixth bowl

[I saw] the sixth angel pour his bowl on the great Euphrates River. Its water was dried up to prepare the way for the kings from the east.

9th Vision in Cycle 7: Three demonic spirits

Then **I saw** three disgusting spirits like frogs come out of the mouth of the dragon, out of the mouth of the beast, and out of the mouth of the false prophet.

Explanation of symbols:

They are demonic spirits that perform signs. They go to the kings of the whole earth and gather them for the war of the great day of God Almighty.

Jesus' exhortation to prepare for his coming

"See, I am coming like a thief. How blessed is the person who remains alert and keeps his clothes on! He won't have to go naked and let others see his shame."

10th Vision in Cycle 7: The demons gather the kings to Armageddon.

---

[a] 16:10 Lit. *They*

The spirits[b] gathered the kings[c] at the place that is called Armageddon in Hebrew.

11th Vision in Cycle 7: the seventh angel with the seventh bowl

[Then I saw] the seventh angel pour his bowl into the air. A loud voice came from the throne in the temple and said,
"It is done!"

There were flashes of lightning, noises, peals of thunder, and a powerful earthquake.

Explanation of vision: The Greek word translated "It is done" can also be translated, "It is finished" or "It is completed." It is another example of each cycle ending with the End of the world.

There has never been such a powerful earthquake since people have been on the earth.

12th Vision in Cycle 7: the city split into three parts

[Then I saw] the great city split into three parts, and the cities of the nations fell.

John's comment

God remembered to give Babylon the Great the cup of wine filled with the fury of his wrath.

13th Vision in Cycle 7: The End of the world; Islands and mountains vanish; mankind is judged; end of Cycle 7

---

[b] 16:16 Lit. *They*

[c] 16:16 Lit. *them*

Every island vanished,[d] and the mountains could no longer be found. [21]Huge hailstones, each weighing about 100 pounds,[e] fell from the sky on people. They cursed God because the plague of hail was such a terrible plague.

Cycle 8 John is now carried to the wilderness

1st Vision in Cycle 8: the judgment of Babylon the Great

Then [I saw] one of the seven angels who held the seven bowls came and said to me,

"Come, I will show you the judgment of the notorious prostitute who sits on many waters. The kings of the earth committed sexual immorality with her, and those living on earth became drunk with the wine of her immorality."

Then the angel[a] carried me away in the Spirit into a wilderness.

2nd Vision in Cycle 8: The Woman rides the beast

I saw a woman sitting on a scarlet beast that was filled with blasphemous names. It had seven heads and ten horns. The woman wore purple and scarlet clothes and was adorned with gold, gems, and pearls. In her hand she was holding a gold cup filled with detestable things and the impurities of her immorality. On her forehead was written a secret name:
BABYLON THE GREAT,
THE MOTHER OF PROSTITUTES
AND DETESTABLE THINGS OF THE EARTH

---

[d] 16:20 Or *fled*

[e] 16:21 Lit. *Huge hailstones about a talent*

[a] 17:3 Lit. *he*

3rd Vision in Cycle 8: The Woman drunk with blood

I saw that the woman was drunk with the blood of the saints and the blood of the witnesses to Jesus.

John's comment

I was very surprised when **I saw** her.

Audio experience: The symbols explained by the angel

The angel said to me,

"Why are you surprised? I will tell you the secret of the woman and the beast with the seven heads and the ten horns that carries her. The beast that you saw once was, is no longer, and is going to come from the bottomless pit and go to its destruction. Those living on earth, whose names were not written in the Book of Life from the foundation of the world, will be surprised when they see the beast because it was, is no longer, and will come again. This calls for a mind that has wisdom. The seven heads are seven mountains on which the woman is sitting. They are also seven kings. Five of them have fallen, one is living, and the other has not yet come. When he comes, he must remain for a little while. The beast that was and is no longer is the eighth king,[b] but it belongs with the seven kings[c] and goes to its destruction. The ten horns that you saw are ten kings who have not yet received a kingdom. They will receive authority to rule[d] as kings with the beast for one hour. They have one purpose: to give their power

---

[b] 17:11 The Gk. lacks *king*

[c] 17:11 The Gk. lacks *kings*

[d] 17:12 The Gk. lacks *to rule*

111

and authority to the beast. They will wage war against the lamb, but the lamb will conquer them because he is Lord of lords and King of kings. Those who are called, chosen, and faithful are with him."

Audio experience: The angel explains more

The angel[e] also said to me,

"The waters you saw, on which the prostitute is sitting, are peoples, multitudes, nations, and languages. The ten horns and the beast you saw will hate the prostitute. They will leave her abandoned and naked. They will eat her flesh and burn her up with fire, for God has put it into their hearts to carry out his purpose. And so they will give their kingdom to the beast until God's words are fulfilled. The woman you saw is the great city that rules over the kings of the earth."

4th Vision in Cycle 8: the Fall of Babylon

After these things **I saw** another angel coming down from heaven. He had great authority,[a] and the earth was made bright by his splendor.

Audio Experience

He cried out in a powerful voice,

"Fallen! Babylon the Great has fallen! She has become a home for demons. She is a prison for every unclean spirit, a prison for every unclean bird, and a prison for every unclean and hated beast. For all the nations have drunk from the wine of her sexual immorality, and the kings of the earth have committed

---

[e] 17:15 Lit. *He*

[a] 18:1 Or *tremendous power*

Byhalia High School
Commencement Exercises

Motto:
"We cannot discover new Oceans
Unless we have the Courage to lose
Sight of the Shore"

Saturday, May 19, 2012
2:00 P.M.
Rust College Gymnasium
Holly Springs, Mississippi

Faculty and Staff

Anderson, Shenise .... Language Arts
Brown, Sterling .... Vocational Agriculture
Cook, Danielle .... Computer Technology
Crenshaw, Chanda .... Mathematics
Crockett, Tony .... Band
Danley, John .... Social Studies
Dixon, Trevan .... Special Education
Duggins, Alexandria .... Mathematics
Endicott, Ann .... Vocational Special Population
Filocco, Stacy .... Foreign Language
Gaulding, Linda .... Vocational Marketing Technology
Hamblin, Deborah .... Library
Hawkins, Jeff .... Drivers Education
Holland, Fred .... Vocational Agricultural Science
Hutchinson, Todd .... Health and Physical Education
Jackson, Don .... Principal
Jenkins, Milony .... Language Arts
Johnson, Jermaine .... Special Education
Johnson, Lonnie .... Mathematics
Kimbrough, Amy .... Administrative Assistant
Lester, Cecil .... Special Education
Martin, Lisa .... Social Studies
McClatchy, Marie .... Administrative Assistant
McClish, Sean .... Chemistry
Mitchell, Sally .... Vocational Consumer Science
Nandrajog, Poonam .... Mathematics
Oliver, William .... Assistant Principal
Pannell, Summer .... Instructional Facilitator, Assistant Principal
Pegues, Leisa .... Special Education
Reed, Melinda .... Language Arts
Riddle, Crystal .... Language Arts
Riddle, Sherman .... Learning Strategies
Sanders, Laslee .... Social Studies
Shannon, Ashley .... Social Studies
Sharp, Felicia .... Counselor
Stewart, Janet .... Special Education
Thomas, LaDonna .... Language Arts
Thompson, Lydia .... Vocational Consumer Science
Taylor, Leora .... Administrative Assistant
Ware, Katrina .... Biology
Washington, Markeith .... Physical Education
Watson, Chris .... Biology
Wilson, Lucinda .... Special Education

Ushers

Sean McClish	Laslee Sanders	Poonam Nandrajog
Lisa Pegues	Chanda Crenshaw	Lisa Martin

Programme

Processional ..... "Pomp and Circumstance" ..... Mr. Tony Crockett

Welcome .... Mr. William Oliver
Assistant Principal

Invocation .... Miss Khadija Craine

Welcome .... Mr. Andrew J. Levin

Class Song .... Senior Class Members

Introduction of Salutatorian .... Miss Turshelia Scruggs
Salutatorian Address .... Miss Alexia Taylor Mazique

Introduction of Valedictorian .... Mr. William J. Ferris, III

Valedictorian Address .... Miss Mariah Lynne Clarkson

Acknowledgement of Honors and Scholarships .... Mr. Fred Holland
Senior Sponsor

Special Recognition .... Mr. Don Jackson
Principal
Class Song .... "I Smile" .... Senior Class Members
Presentation of Graduates .... Miss Felicia Sharp
Counselor
Pronouncement of Graduates .... Mr. Jerry Moore
Superintendent of the Marshall County School District

Presentation of Certificates and Diplomas .... Mr. Don Jackson
Miss Summer Pannell
Miss Felicia Sharp

Declaration of Graduation .... Mr. Don Jackson

Benediction .... Mr. Jalen Applewhite

Recessional .... "Pomp and Circumstance" .... Band
Byhalia High School

Senior Class 2012

Mariah Lynne Clarkson***
Alexia Taylor Mazique**#
Andrew Joseph Levin*
Kristin L. Randall*
Nastarcia S. Owens* #
Jalen J. Applewhite*#
Turshelia Kerra Scruggs*#
Danielle s. Rayford*
Kianna Sheree Sessom*#
Aniqua Trinee Harris*#
Taneisha Shamae Beard*#
Deonta C. Barnum
Martavius Montae Brown@
Luis Javier Cardenas
John S. Chea
Aramis Jordan Cooper
Edgar Cordero
Khadija Zynea Craine
Sofia L. Cruz
Jamal Danley
Darius Kyree Davis
Terrica Lynn Davis @
Carderious Dean
Kadega C. Dowdy
Dakota J. Downs
Jamerson D. Euell
Mi'landrick Tavaris Falkner
Godfrey Fayne
William John Ferris, III
Tieara Ford
Cory German
Quanisha Vontae Grayson
Carnell B. Hall
Pedro L. Hawk, Jr.
Casey Steven Hopper
Jasmine K. Jackson#
Shakedra B. Jackson
Clarivel Jaramillo
Lakelsa A. Jeffries
Shelby M. Johnson@
Bianca Marshea Jones

Darian Desjaim Jones
Latara JaQuay Jones
Lavatta D. Jones
Myesha M. Lawson@
Amanda Lyles
Coraunta L. Martin
Miguel A. Martinez
Allie Maria Milam
Demetrius C. Milam
Tierra S. Moore
Ashie Gwen Mosley
Tia Marie Neeley
Jessica M. Newsom
Lilsy E. Ordaz
Christopher T. Osborne
Dustyn C. Patterson
Jameka Nicole Perkins
Teresa Phillips@
Shanelle L. Rayford
Keion D. Reed
Corey James Richardson
Ambrisha Mesha Richmond
Corterris C. Richmond
Reginald Richmond
Edwardo Rodriguez
Brittney Denae Rosenbaum@
Joshua Tyler Rosenbaum
Carmen S. Saulsberry@
Gracie M. Scroggins
Johathan Kentrell Shipp
Shidrica P. Smith
Shaquille Stanback
Cameron X. Stewart
Edward Stewart
Alisha S. Street@
Tavoris D. Watkins
Harold W. Wilson
Madarria L. Wilson
Ca'Nesha S. Woods
Zinna S. Woods
Kaitlyn M. Yielding

******

***Valedictorian   **Salutatorian   *Gold Cord – Honor Students
@ Blue Stole –DECA Club   +Blue & Gold – FFA Club   #Black & Gold – Bata Club

sexual immorality with her. The merchants of the earth have become rich from the power of her luxury."
Audio Experience

Then **I heard** another voice from heaven saying,

"Come out of her, my people, so that you don't participate in her sins and suffer from her plagues. For her sins are piled as high as heaven, and God has remembered her crimes. Do to her as she herself has done. Give her double for her deeds. Mix a double drink for her in the cup she mixed. Just as she glorified herself and lived in luxury, so give her just as much torture and misery. In her heart she says, "I am a queen on a throne, not a widow. I will never see misery."

For this reason her plagues of death, misery, and famine will come in a single day.She will be burned up in a fire, because powerful is the Lord God who judges her."

Symbols Explained: The End Judgment has now come upon her

The kings of the earth, who committed sexual immorality with her and lived in luxury with her, will cry and mourn over her when they see the smoke rising from her fire. Frightened by her torture, they will stand far away and say,

"How terrible, how terrible it is for that great city, the powerful city Babylon! For in one hour **your judgment has come**!"

Comment inserted: The reaction of her clients

The merchants of the earth cry and mourn over her, because no one buys their cargo anymore— cargo of gold, silver, gems, pearls, fine linen, purple cloth, silk, scarlet cloth, all kinds of scented wood, all articles made of ivory, all articles made of very costly wood, bronze, iron, marble, cinnamon, spice, incense, myrrh, frankincense, wine, olive oil, flour, wheat, cattle, sheep, horses, chariots, and slaves (that is, human souls).

Audio experience continued

"The fruit for which your soul craved has left you. All your dainties and your splendor are lost to you. No one will ever find them again."

Comments inserted

Frightened by her torture, the merchants of these wares who had become rich from her will stand far away. They will cry and mourn, ¹⁶saying,

"How terrible, how terrible it is for the great city that was clothed in fine linen, purple, and scarlet and was adorned with gold, gems, and pearls! For in one hour all this wealth has been destroyed!"

Comments inserted

Every ship's captain, everyone who traveled by ship, sailors, and everyone who made a living by the sea stood far away.
When they saw the smoke from her fire, they began to cry out,
"What city was like the great city?"
Then they threw dust on their heads and shouted while crying and mourning,

"How terrible, how terrible it is for the great city, where all who had ships at sea became rich because of her wealth! For in one hour she has been destroyed! Gloat over her, heaven, saints, apostles, and prophets! For God has condemned her for you."

5th Vision in Cycle 8: a powerful angel with the millstone

Then [I saw] a powerful angel picks up a stone that was like a large millstone and throw it into the sea, saying,

"The great city Babylon will be thrown down with violent force— and will never be found again. The sound of harpists, musicians, flutists, and trumpeters will never be heard in you again. No artisan of any trade will ever be found in you again. The sound of a Millstone will never be heard in you again. The light from a lamp will never shine in you again. The voice of a bridegroom and bride will never be heard in you again for your merchants were the important people of the world, and all the nations were deceived by your witchcraft. The blood of prophets, saints, and all who had been murdered on earth was found in her."

Audio Experience: The End Judgment described.

After these things **I heard** what sounded like the loud voice of a large crowd in heaven, saying,

"Hallelujah! Salvation, glory, and power belong to our God. His judgments are true and just. He has condemned the notorious prostitute who corrupted the world with her immorality. He has taken revenge on her for the blood of his servants."

Audio experience: Cycle 8 closes with the End taking place

A second time they said,

"Hallelujah! The smoke goes up from her forever and ever."

Cycle 8 ends with the final judgment.

Cycle 9 begins

John is translated from earth to heaven.

1st Vision in Cycle 9: The 24 elders

Then [I saw] twenty-four elders and the four living creatures bowed down and worshiped God, who was sitting on the throne. They said,

"Amen! Hallelujah!"

Audio Experience

A voice came from the throne, **saying**,

"Praise our God, all who serve and fear him, from the least important to the most important."

Another audio experience

Then **I heard** what sounded like the voice of a large crowd, like the sound of raging waters, and like the sound of powerful thunderclaps, saying,

"Hallelujah! The Lord our God, the Almighty, is reigning. Let us rejoice, be glad, and give him glory because the marriage of the lamb has come and his bride has made herself ready. She has been given the privilege of wearing fine linen, dazzling and pure."

John explains the symbols.

The fine linen represents the righteous deeds of the saints.

116

Audio experience starts up again.

Then the angel[a] **said** to me,

"Write this: How blessed are those who are invited to the marriage supper of the lamb!'"

He also **told** me,

"These are the true words of God."

John inserts a personal note about his mistake of trying to worship the angel as a warning to his readers.

I bowed down at his feet to worship him, but he told me, "Don't do that! I am a fellow servant with you and with your brothers who hold on to the testimony of Jesus. Worship God, because the testimony of Jesus is the spirit of prophecy!"

2nd Vision in Cycle 9: the Second Coming of Christ

Then **I saw** heaven standing open, and there was a white horse! Its rider is named Faithful and True, and in righteousness he judges and wages war. His eyes are like a flame of fire, and on his head are many royal crowns. He has a name written on him that nobody knows except himself. He is dressed in a robe dipped in[b] blood, and his name is called the Word of God.

3rd Vision in Cycle 9: The Armies of heaven

---

[a] 19:9 Lit. *he*

[b] 19:13 Other mss. read *sprinkled with*

Then [I saw] the armies of heaven, wearing fine linen, white and pure, follow him on white horses. A sharp sword comes out of his mouth to strike down the nations.

He will rule^c them with an iron rod and tread the winepress of the fury of the wrath of God Almighty. On his robe and his thigh he has a name written:

KING OF KINGS AND LORD OF LORDS

4th Vision in Cycle 9: the Angel's Gathering of the vultures

Then **I saw** an angel standing in the sun. He cried out in a loud voice to all the birds flying overhead,

"Come! Gather for the great supper of God. Eat the flesh of kings, the flesh of commanders, the flesh of warriors,^d the flesh of horses and their riders, and the flesh of all people, both free and slaves, both unimportant and important."

5th Vision in Cycle 9: Judgment of the Beast, the False Prophet, and those who followed them

Then **I saw** the beast, the kings of the earth, and their armies gathered to wage war against the rider on the horse and his army. The beast was captured, along with the false prophet who had performed signs on its behalf.^e By these signs^f the false prophet^g had deceived those who had received the mark of the

---

^c 19:15 Or *shepherd*

^d 19:18 Lit. *of the powerful*

^e 19:20 Or *in its presence*

^f 19:20 Lit. *By which*

^g 19:20 Lit. *he*

beast and worshiped its image. Both of them were thrown alive into the lake of fire that burns with sulfur. The rest were killed by the sword that belonged to the rider on the horse and that came from his mouth. And all the birds gorged themselves on their flesh.

End of Cycle 9 with the final judgment of mankind, the beast and the false prophet by the returning Messiah.

Cycle Ten

The End is recast from the viewpoint of heaven.

1st Vision in Cycle 10: The capture and restraint of the dragon

Then **I saw** an angel coming down from heaven, holding the key to the bottomless pit and a large chain in his hand. He captured the dragon, that ancient serpent, who is the devil and Satan, and tied him up for a thousand years. He threw him into the bottomless pit, locked it, and sealed it over him to keep him from deceiving the nations anymore until the thousand years were over. After that he must be set free for a little while.

2nd Vision in Cycle 10: heavenly thrones for those who will judge the earth

⁴Then **I saw** thrones, and those who sat on them were given authority to judge.

3rd Vision in Cycle 10: the souls of martyrs on heavenly thrones.

I also saw the souls of those who had been beheaded because of their testimony about Jesus and because of the word of God.

John's explanation of why they honored.

They had not worshiped the beast or its image and had not received its mark on their foreheads or hands.

John explains their reward.

They came back to life and ruled with Christ for a thousand years.

4th Vision in Cycle 10: The fate of the rest of the dead

Then [I saw] that the rest of the dead did not come back to life until the thousand years were over. This is the first resurrection.

John inserts an explanation and exhortation

How blessed and holy are those who participate in the first resurrection! The second death has no power over them. They will be priests of God and Christ, and will rule with him for a thousand years.

5th Vision in Cycle 10: the freeing and final defeat of Satan, the final battle, and eternal punishment.

[And I saw] when the thousand years are over, Satan will be freed from his prison. He will go out to deceive Gog and Magog, the nations at the four corners of the earth, and gather them for war. They are as numerous as the sands of the seashore. They marched over the broad expanse of the earth and surrounded the camp of the saints and the beloved city. Fire came from God[a] out of heaven and burned them up, and the devil who

---

[a] 20:9 Other mss. lack *from God*

deceived them was thrown into the lake of fire and sulfur, where the beast and the false prophet were. They will be tortured day and night forever and ever.

6th Vision in Cycle 10: the White Throne Judgment

Then **I saw** a large, white throne and the one who was sitting on it.

7th Vision in Cycle 10: heaven and earth vanish

Then [I saw] earth and the heavens fled from his presence, and no place was found for them.

8th Vision in Cycle 10: The dead judged

Then **I saw** the dead, both unimportant and important, standing in front of the throne, and books were open. Another book was opened—the Book of Life. The dead were judged according to their works, as recorded in the books. The sea gave up the dead that were in it, and Death and Hades[b] gave up the dead that were in them, and all were judged according to their works. Death and Hades[c] were thrown into the lake of fire. This is the second death—the lake of fire. Anyone whose name was not found written in the Book of Life was thrown into the lake of fire.

9th Vision in Cycle 10: a new heaven and a new earth

End of Cycle 10 with the final judgment.

Cycle Eleven

---

[b] 20:13 I.e. the realm of the dead

[c] 20:14 I.e. the realm of the dead

Then **I saw** a new heaven and a new earth, because the first heaven and the first earth had disappeared, and the sea was gone.

1st Vision in Cycle 11: the holy city descends down from heaven

I also saw the holy city, New Jerusalem, coming down from God out of heaven, prepared like a bride adorned for her husband.

Audio experience

I **heard** a loud voice from the throne say,

"See, the tabernacle of God is among humans! He will make his home with them, and they will be his people. God himself will be with them, and he will be their God.[a] He will wipe every tear from their eyes. There won't be death anymore. There won't be any grief, crying, or pain, because the first things have disappeared."

Another audio experience:

The one sitting on the throne said,

"See, I am making all things new!"

He **said**,

"Write this:
'These words are trustworthy and true.'"

Then he **said** to me,

---

[a] 21:3 Other mss. lack *and he will be their God*

"It has happened! I am the Alpha and the Omega, the beginning and the end. I will freely give a drink from the spring of the water of life to the one who is thirsty. The person who conquers will inherit these things. I will be his God, and he will be my son. But people who are cowardly, unfaithful, detestable, murderers, sexually immoral, sorcerers, idolaters, and all liars will find themselves in[b] the lake that burns with fire and sulfur. This is the second death."

End of Cycle 11

Cycle Twelve

John is now taken from heaven to view the New Jerusalem.
1st Vision in Cycle 12: The angel show John the Bride of Messiah
:

Then one of the seven angels who had the seven bowls full of the seven last plagues came to me and **said,**

"Come! I will **show** you the bride, the wife of the lamb."

2nd Vision in Cycle 12: the Holy City

He carried me away in the Spirit to a large, high mountain and **showed** me the holy city, Jerusalem, coming down from God out of heaven.

John describes what he saw:

It had the glory of God, and its light was like a valuable gem, like jasper, as clear as crystal. It had a large, high wall with twelve gates. Twelve angels were at the gates, and the names of the twelve tribes of Israel were written on the gates. There were three gates on the east, three gates on the north, three gates on the

---

[b] 21:8 Lit. *will have their part in*

south, and three gates on the west. The wall of the city had twelve foundations, and the twelve names of the twelve apostles of the lamb were written on them.

3rd Vision in Cycle 12: The measuring of the temple

Then [I saw] the angel who[c] was **talking** to me had a gold measuring rod to measure the city, its gates, and its walls. [16]The city was square: its length was the same as its width. He measured the city with his rod, and it was about 1,374 miles long.[d] Its length, width, and height were the same. He also measured its wall. According to the human measurement that the angel was using it was 252 feet.[e] Its wall was made of jasper. The city was made of pure gold, as clear as glass. The foundations of the city wall were decorated with all kinds of gems: The first foundation[f] was jasper, the second sapphire, the third agate, the fourth emerald, the fifth onyx, the sixth carnelian, the seventh chrysolite, the eighth beryl, the ninth topaz, the tenth chrysoprase, the eleventh jacinth, and the twelfth amethyst. The twelve gates were twelve pearls, and each gate was made of a single pearl. The street of the city was made of pure gold, as clear as glass.

I saw no temple in it, because the Lord God Almighty and the lamb are its temple.

The city doesn't need any sun or moon to give it light, because the glory of God gave it light, and the lamb was its lamp. The nations will walk in its light, and the kings of the earth will bring their glory into it. Its gates will never be shut by day,

---

[c] 21:15 Lit. *The one who*

[d] 21:16 Lit. *12,000 stadia*; The Roman mile contained eight stadia, one stadion was about 604.5 feet long.

[e] 21:17 Lit. *144 cubits*; The royal cubit was about 20-one inches long.

[f] 21:19 The Gk. lacks *foundation*

because there won't be any night there. People[g] will bring the glory and wealth[h] of the nations into it. Nothing unclean, or anyone who does anything detestable, and no one who tells lies will ever enter it. Only those whose names[i] are written in the lamb's Book of Life will enter it.[j]

4th Vision in Cycle 12: the River of the Water of Life

Then the angel[a] **showed** me the river of the water of life, as clear as crystal. It was flowing from the throne of God and the lamb. Between the street of the city and the river there was the tree of life visible from both sides. It produced twelve kinds of fruit, each month having its own fruit. The leaves of the tree are for the healing of the nations. There will no longer be any curse. The throne of God and the lamb will be in the city.[b] His servants will worship him and see his face, and his name will be on their foreheads. There will be no more night, and they will not need any light from lamps or the sun because the Lord God will shine on them. They will rule forever and ever.

Audio Experience

He **said** to me,

---

[g] 21:26 Lit. *They*

[h] 21:26 Or *honor*

[i] 21:27 Lit. *those who*

[j] 21:27 The Gk. lacks *will enter it*

[a] 22:1 Lit. *he*

[b] 22:3 Lit. *in it*

"These words are trustworthy and true. The Lord God of the spirits and of the prophets has sent his angel to show his servants the things that must happen soon."

Jesus inserts a promise.

"See! I am coming soon! How blessed is the person who keeps the words of the prophecy in this book!"

Cycle 12 ends

Epilogue and Benediction by John

I, John, **heard and saw** these things.

John attempts to worship the angel but is corrected.

When I had **heard and seen** them, I bowed down to worship at the feet of the angel who had been showing me these things. But he told me,

"Don't do that! I am a fellow servant with you, your brothers the prophets, and those who keep the words in this book. Worship God!"

Then he said to me,
"Don't seal up the words of the prophecy in this book, because the time is near. Let the one who does what is evil continue to do evil, and let the filthy person continue to be filthy, and the righteous person continue to do what is right, and the holy person continue to be holy."

The Messiah now dictates His concluding words to John.

"See! I am coming soon! My reward is with me to repay everyone according to his work. I am the Alpha and the

Omega, the first and the last, the beginning and the end.[c]
How blessed are those who wash their robes[d] so that they
may have the right to the tree of life and may go through
the gates into the city! Outside are dogs, sorcerers, immoral
people, murderers, idolaters, and everyone who loves and
practices falsehood. I, Jesus, have sent my angel to give
this testimony to you for the churches. I am the root and
descendent of David, the bright morning star."

Audio experience: The Spirit and the Church invites sinners to
come to Messiah for salvation.

The Spirit and the bride say, "Come!"
Let everyone who hears this say, "Come!"
Let everyone who is thirsty come!
Let anyone who wants the water of life take it as a gift!

John warms his readers:

"I warn everyone who hears the words of the prophecy in
this book:
If anyone adds anything to them, God will strike him with
the plagues that are written in this book.
If anyone takes away any words from the book of this
prophecy,
God will take away his portion of the tree of life and the
holy city that are described in this book."

Jesus Speaks:

The One who is testifying to these things says,

---

[c] 22:13 The speaker possibly concludes his quotation here rather than at the end
of vs. 16.

[d] 22:14 Other mss. read *who do his commandments*

"Yes, I am coming soon!"

John's response to Jesus' promise to return: He prays to Jesus and asks him to come back.

"Amen!
Come, Lord Jesus!"

John's closing benediction:

May the grace of the Lord Jesus be with all the saints. Amen.[f]

<hr>

[f] 22:21 Other mss. lack *Amen*

Chapter Two

Modern Western European Approaches

Our first task is to get rid of all the cultural baggage we have inherited from modern Western European approaches to the Book of Revelation. Western European scholars have approached the Apocalypse with many cultural assumptions that hindered their interpretation of this first century Jewish apocalyptic work. Typical Western approaches include:

A. Total Preterism: This view includes liberal and conservative scholars who feel that the Apocalypse had only in view the immediate circumstances of the author, such as the Roman Empire, its emperors, its persecutions of believers, the destruction of the temple, and the hope of divine deliverance. Thus, the Apocalypse is reduced to the immediate situation and has nothing to do with the End of the world. It is an example of theological reductionism.

Liberal Preterists assume that John and the infant Church in general were all mistaken in the belief that Jesus was going to return in their lifetime to destroy the Roman Empire and deliver Israel from the yoke of tyranny. This error came from Jesus himself, who mistakenly thought he would come back right away. The Apocalypse is solid proof that Jesus was not a divine Messiah.

Conservative Preterists generally follow the commentaries written by liberal Preterists. They too see all the events covered in the Apocalypse as fulfilled in the immediate historical context of John. Thus, the Second Coming, the Resurrection, the final Judgments of angels and men, eternal torment, etc. were all fulfilled at the destruction of the temple in A. D. 70 by the Roman general Titus.

Conservative Preterists at first do not follow the liberals all the way down the path of perdition and end up denying the Trinity, the deity of Christ, etc. They would never say that Jesus was mistaken in his beliefs. But down through the years, most of the total Preterists I have personally known eventually ended up denying the Trinity. It is just a matter of time before they follow their liberal hermeneutic to its eventual end.

The main problem with this modern Western Gentile hermeneutic is that the Old Testament prophets, intertestamental Jewish Apocalypticism, the apostles, and Jesus were not Preterists. They were futurists because they foresaw the future coming of the Messiah as taking place at the End of the world and did not see it as fulfilled by some event in their own time and situation. Thus while they would speak of events in their own day in terminology of the End, to emphasize their importance in God's plan of history, they did not think that those immediate events fulfilled the End. For example, the Flood was described with imagery and language drawn from the End for poetic and dramatic effect (Mat. 24:37-38, etc.) But, after the Flood, the prophets continued to speak of the End because the Flood did not literally fulfill the End time prophecies.

While the Flood, the Tower, the Judgments on Egypt, the Exodus, the Conquest of Canaan, the Assyrian and Babylonian Captivities, the Return of Israel, the rebuilding of the temple, and its various destructions could all be described with vivid imagery drawn from the prophecies concerning the End of the world, none of those events were literal fulfillments of the End.

In the same way, the destruction of the temple in A.D. 70 was indeed described with imagery drawn from the End (Mat. 24). But it should not be interpreted as the literal fulfillment of the End any more than the Flood was the fulfillment of the End.

When you go to a theater to see a movie, you will first see "previews of coming attractions." Are these "previews" the coming movies? No. In the same way, many events in biblical history were *previews* of the coming attractions" that will surround the End. Preterists confuse the previews with the End itself.

B. Partial Preterism: Some conservative scholars understand that any denial of the Second Coming of Christ, the bodily Resurrection of the righteous and the wicked, the Judgment Day, and the eternal bliss or eternal torment awaiting angels and men is a damnable heresy. But, due to a faulty interpretation of the Mt. Olivet discourse, they think that the Preterists are right to some extent.

C. Historism: The Apocalypse has in view the entire age of church history and has been fulfilled here and there by various politicians such as Nero or religious leaders such as the Catholic Popes. The Reformers were so convinced the Pope was the anti-Christ that they wrote this view into their creeds and confessions. Many of the standard Protestant commentaries on Revelation reflect the Reformation view. Most Post-Millenialists and A-Millenialists would identify themselves as belonging to historistic approach to Revelation.

D. Idealism: This classic liberal view avoids any attempt to find fulfillments of the Apocalypse in past, present, or future history. Instead, it emphasizes the eternal cosmic conflict between good and evil that is supposedly found in all ancient cosmologies.

E. Futurism: This approach comes in so many different forms today that we are tempted to throw up our hands in despair that so many conflicting systems can be legitimately brought under this one rubric.

Many futurists are as guilty of theological reductionism as the Preterists. They reduce the Apocalypse to the final period of history just preceding the Return of Christ. They do not see any relevance to the immediate circumstances of John or the early Church. But the choice is not between everything in the Apocalypse is past or everything is future. Theological extremes are seldom right. The distinctive features that run through all futuristic interpretations of the Apocalypse are as follows:

> 1. All or most of the Book of Revelation concerns the End of the world.

2. Many see the seven churches as a prophetic blueprint of seven successive ages of church history from beginning to the End.

3. Each generation of futurists identifies itself as the Laodicean church/age.

4. Others see the seven churches as dealing with seven real churches and not prophetic *per se*. They are a historical prelude to prophecy and not prophecy.

5. The End is upon us today.

6. Each generation is convinced that it is the terminal generation.

7. It is possible to identify contemporary events and people as literal fulfillments of the things predicted in Revelation.

8. In the recent past, WWII, Hitler, Mussolini, Russia, Communism, the European Commonwealth, Mao, Prince Charles, Gorbachev, Kissinger, U.S. Presidents such as Richard Nixon, Ronald Reagan, Bill Clinton, Obama, and the Bushes, Bill Gates, various popes, etc. have all been identified as the anti-Christ or the false prophet.

9. A linear hermeneutic which assumes that the visions in Revelations should be lined up like ducks in a row and that each one is a separate event In the future.

10. A tendency to set dates for the Rapture, the Second Coming or the End. In recent times 1975, 1984, 1994, and 2,000 were chosen as the End of the world.

F. Dispensational Pre-Tribulational Pre-Millennialism, and Historic Mid-Tribulational or Post-Tribulational Pre-Millennialism have dominated American Evangelicalism for many years and is often used by some colleges and seminaries to keep liberals from becoming professors. Since we deal with the errors of Dispensationalism in the book, *How the Old and New Testaments Relate to Each Other* (www.faithdefenders.com), we will explore its many conflicting theological systems and it hermeneutical flaws.

Conclusion

Our approach to the Apocalypse is not the typical Western European hermeneutic. Instead, it begins with the assumption that since the Apocalypse is a first century Jewish work, it must be interpreted according to the way apocalyptic literature was understood by Jews in the first century. For this reason in the next chapter will give a summary of Apocalyptic hermeneutics.

In contrast, those use a modern Western European hermeneutical system and artificially apply it to such ancient Jewish literature as the Apocalypse, they can never figure out what is happening. Modern approaches are more European than Middle Eastern, more Gentile than Jewish, and more modern than first century. To apply modern hermeneutics to a first century Apocalypse is the cause of much mischief and controversy.

Chapter Three

Jewish Apocalypticism

Introduction

When you begin to read the Bible for the first time, you soon run across bizarre passages that use weird images. Cosmic battles will take place in heaven and on earth. Is this sci-fi stuff or is it for real? A huge red dragon with seven heads, ten horns, and seven crowns comes out of the sea. Is the Bible saying that Godzilla is for real?

There are weird creatures with body parts from insects, animals, and man. An angel grabs the dragon and puts a chain on him and then opens a hole in the ground and throws him in it. Is the Bible talking about literal chains, dragons, and holes in the ground? Or, are all those things symbolic images of something else? How do we interpret those kinds of passages?

Part I

The following propositions are meant to give us a bird's eye view of the issues involved in interpreting prophetic passages in the Bible.

1.   *The failure to begin with the Bible as literature is the chief source of most of the nonsense and heresy that is passed off today as "Bible prophecy."* Too many people assume that the Bible is *one* book that can be interpreted by *one* hermeneutical principle such as literalism. This false assumption has spawned thousands of apocalyptic cults (i.e. Jehovah's Witnesses) as well as having misled sincere

Christians.

The "Bible" is a collection of 66 ancient Jewish scrolls written by over forty men during a two thousand year process. It is composed of many different kinds or genres of literature. There are historical narratives, poetry, hymns, theological discourses, and prophetic passages that talk about the near and distant future of men and nations and even about the End of the world.

2.   *Each type or genre of literature found in the Bible must be interpreted according to its own unique historical, cultural, religious, and literary context.* The failure to do so results in eisegesis (i.e. the reading of one's own subjective ideas into the text of Scripture), instead of exegesis (the digging out of the text the objective ideas that the author of that text was trying to convey to his readers).

3.   *The goal of Biblical studies is to discover what the authors of the Bible were saying to the people of their day.* The reason why this is important is that they were not simply giving their own private opinion on things but they spoke from Divine inspiration (2 Peter 1:20-21). In other words, their opinion was God's opinion! This is why it is wrong to obscure their message by inserting your own ideas into their documents.

4.   *The last book in the Bible is entitled by its author as "The <u>Apocalypse</u> of Jesus Christ" (1:1).* When the KJV changed the title to *"The Revelation of St. John the Divine"*, it obscured the nature of the book.

5.   *The Greek word "apocalypse" at that time meant the "unveiling" of hidden mysteries concerning the future as it relates to the ultimate outcome of the final battle between good and evil at the End of the world.*

6.   *The word "apocalyptic" became a literary and theological term to describe any literature that "unveiled" the End of the world.* Hence, the word "apocalyptic" is applied to other Biblical books and passages. The following is a list of some of the books and passages found in the Bible.

Old Testament Material

Isaiah 65 – 66	Ezekiel 38 – 42	Daniel	Zechariah 12 – 14

New Testament Material

Book	Chp/Ver	Book	Chp/Ver	Book	Chp/Ver	Book	Chp/Ver
Matt.	3:7-10	Mark	1:15	Luke	1:32-33	Juan	5:25-29
	5:17 / 6:10		9:10-13		10:12-15		
	7:21-22 /		12:18-24		12:4-5, 35-53		
	11:15, 22-24		13		17:22-37		
	12:36-37				20:27-38		
	13:24-30				21:5-23		
	36-43						
	47-50						
	16:27-28						
	19:28-30						
	22:29-31						
	24-25						
Acts	1:11	Romans	11	1 Cor.	15	Phi. 1	3:20-21

3:19-20				
1 Thes 4:13-18	2 Thes	2	1 Tim. 6:14-16	Titus 2:13
5:1-11				
Hebrews 9:28	2 Peter	3	1 John 3:2-3	Jude
Reveletaion				

7. *In the last fifty years, an enormous amount of ancient documents have been discovered in Israel that date from 250 BC to AD 200.* Some of these documents are written in the same genre as the books of Daniel and Revelation and are clearly "apocalyptic" in nature. While we do not consider them inspired or part of the canon of Scripture, they do have great historical and literary value.

The following is a list of some of these works that in part or in whole have been classified as "apocalyptic." To the list below we also add The Dead Sea Qumran Community's Commentaries on Isaiah, Hosea, Micah, Nahum, Habakkuk, Zephaniah, and Psalms 37. While they are not apocalyptic *per se*, they do have Cycles that are clearly apocalyptic in nature.

I Enoch
II Enoch
The Testament of the 12 Patriarchs
The Psalms of Solomon
The Assumption of Moses
The Martyrdom of Isaiah
The Book of Jubilees
The Testament of Abraham
The Apocalypse of Moses
The Apocalypse of Abraham
The Sibyline Oracles III, IV, V
II Esdra (or 4 Ezra)
II Baruch
III Baruch
The Zadokite Document
The Manual of Discipline
The Rule of the Congregation
A Scroll of Benedictions
The Messianic Anthology
Hymns of Thanksgiving
The War Scroll
The Book of Mysteries
A Midrash on the Last Days
The New Jerusalem
An Angelic Liturgy
The Prayer of Nabonidus
Pseudo-Daniel Apocalypse
A Genesis Apocryphon
The Testament of Levi

8.   *These ancient documents reveal aspects of the religious context in which Christianity arose and prospered.* Jesus and the Apostles did not step off a UFO one day. They spoke in the context of the religious, political, and cultural situation of their day.

9.   *When we interpret the "apocalyptic" Cycles of the*

New Testament, we must take into account the extra-biblical "apocalyptic" books that came into existence before, during, and after the New Testament was written. These books form the religious, political, and cultural context in which the New Testament was produced. They give us clear indications as to how and why Christianity was transformed from being a minor Jewish sect called "The Way" (Acts 19:9, 23) to a major world religion.

10.   *Almost without exception, "prophecy experts" ignore the Jewish apocalyptic context of the New Testament.* As a result, they insert modern, Gentile, European, and American ideas into the first century Jewish documents called the "New Testament." They assume that prophetic passages should be interpreted the same way as historical narratives, i.e. literal.

11.   *This is why most "prophecy experts" arbitrarily identify contemporary events, individuals, and nations as the fulfillment of End time prophecies.* For example, during World War II, Hitler was frequently identified as the Antichrist. The fact that he did not turn out to be the Antichrist and that WWII did not turn out to be Armageddon has not deterred them from going on to name new individuals such as Henry Kissenger, John Rockefeller, Prince Charles, Ronald Reagan, Saddam Hussein, Bill Clinton or Obama. The identity of the Antichrist changes so often that an "Antichrist of the month club" should be started to see who is on the hit list this month.

12.   *If Church history after the New Testament is important to our understanding of the apocalyptic Cycles of the New Testament, then Jewish history before and during the formation of the New Testament is even more important.* We are not aware of any "Pre", "Post", or "A" Millennial books that begin with a discussion of the nature and significance of apocalyptic literature as it bears on

interpreting prophetic Cycles in the Bible.

13.   *If it is objected that Christians should ignore the apocalyptic literature because it is* Jewish, *it must be pointed out that:*

a.   It was the early Christian Church that preserved these works. They were quoted universally throughout the Early Church. We would not have these works except that the early Christians copied, read, and cherished them.

b.   The early Christians went on to write their own distinctively "Christian" apocalyptic works. The following is a list of the apocalyptic works that appeared early in the history of the Church. They reveal that the average Christian was apocalyptic in his views of the future.

The Didache (16)
The Shepherd of Hermes
The Ascension of Isaiah
The Fifth and Sixth Books of Ezra
The Christian Sibyllines
The Book of Elchasai
The Apocalypse of Peter
Apocalypse of Sophonias
Apocalypse of Elijah
Apocalypse of Zechariah
Apocalypse of John
Apocalypse of Mary
Apocalypse of Stephen
Apocalypse of Bartholomew
Apocalypse of Paul
Apocalypse of Thomas

14.   The following questions must be answered:

(1) *WHY did Jewish rabbis abandon Apocalypticism after AD 70?*
That they did abandon it is clear from three things:

   a.   They did not preserve the pre-Christian apocalyptic literature.

   b.   They did not write any more literature in that style.

   c.   Even though elements of Apocalypticism can be found in the Talmuds, there is a general hostility to it.

(2) *Why did the early Church take over the apocalyptic movement from Judaism?*
That the Church did so is clear from three things:

   a.   The Church preserved the Jewish apocalyptic literature.

   b.   It went on to write more books in that genre.

   c.   Down through the centuries Apocalypticism has been kept alive mainly by Christians. Without the undercurrent of Apocalypticism in the Church, the so-called "prophecy experts" would have gone out of business long ago.

   The two questions above are answered as follows:
   First century Judaism had many sects or denominations. Within Jewish orthodoxy there were two major movements:

   d.   There were *legalistic* groups who promoted the idea

that it is through the keeping of the Torah that salvation will come. They assumed that all revelation ceased since Malachi and that external conformity to the laws of Moses was all that God required. The Pharisees are singled out in the Gospels and in Galatians as examples of this school.

After the Temple was destroyed in AD 70, the Pharisees took over the guardianship of Judaism and they were the ones who wrote the Midrash, the Mishnah, and the Talmuds. Modern Orthodox Judaism is the modern heir of the Pharisees.

e.   The second movement within Orthodox Judaism was the *apocalyptic* movement. They, like the legalists, held the Torah in high regard. But, unlike them, they were open to new revelations. They were expecting the Messiah to come and then return to Glory. They felt that they were in the "last days" foretold by the prophets.

15.   The apocalyptic movement was characterized by the following beliefs:

a.   All things are predestined by God and will happen according to His eternal plan. History is thus linear and has a beginning and an end. There is no such thing as chance or luck.

b.   The world is doomed to get worse and worse.

c.   The wicked will become bolder in persecuting the saints in the last days.

d.   At the last moment, God will intervene through sending the Messiah, the "Son of Man" referred to in Daniel, to defeat the forces of evil.

e.   There will be a final battle in heaven between the Devil and his angels and Michael and his angels. The elect angels will win.

f.   There will also be a final battle on earth between

Israel and the Gentile nations. The chosen people will win.

g. There will be a bodily resurrection of all men.

h. All men will be judged by King Messiah.

i. The reprobate will be thrown in eternal fire where they will be tormented forever.

j. The earth will be cleansed by fire.

k. A new earth and new heavens will be created.

l. Messiah's kingdom shall be eternal.

16. *The main source of converts in the Palestinian Church came from those Jews involved in apocalyptic movement.* While the Pharisees, the Sadducees, Herodians, Zealots, etc., were all enemies of Jesus and the Church, the apocalyptic minded Jews were open to the idea that the Messiah had come because they believed that they were living in the "last days." They were open to *new* revelations, and thus had no problem accepting the New Testament being inspired.

17. *The Pharisees saw the apocalyptic movement flowing into the Church and this is why they decided to abandon apocalyptic literature as a genre and to repudiate the apocalyptic movement that produced them.* To this day, modern Judaism is still hostile to its own tradition of Messianic expectations. Many Rabbis now pretend that the Old Testament verses identified by the New Testament as Messianic in nature were never interpreted that way before by Judaism. This is either complete ignorance or willful deception on their part. I document this in the book, *The Trinity: Evidence and Issues* (www.faithdefenders.com).

18. *Given the above facts, we must still resist the temptation to reduce Christianity to mere Jewish Apocalypticism. Christianity influenced Apocalypticism more than Apocalypticism influenced Christianity.* Christianity took the apocalyptic movement and radically

transformed it by rooting it in such *historical* events as the Incarnation, death, burial, and resurrection of the Messiah. These historical events became the basis of their expectation of final victory at the End of history. The Gospel message looks *back* to the cross as well as *forward* to the crown. Salvation is not earned by observing the Torah. It is a gift of God's grace by virtue of the atonement that Jesus paid on the cross.

19.   *The future victory over evil was now secure because Jesus conquered Satan.* He took the keys of hell and death away from the devil and now wears them on his belt. The kingdom of the Messiah is both *now* a present spiritual reality and *later* a physical manifestation on a new earth. His present kingdom is the *rule* of God in the hearts of men and, after the END, it will be the *realm* where His rule is universal, complete, final, and eternal for "of his kingdom there shall be no end." (Luke 1:33)

Part II

We will now set forth those hermeneutical principles that should be utilized when interpreting apocalyptic literature.

1. *There are times when a biblical prophet was not talking about End time events but about future events that would transpire during this age. Yet, because these events are so significant and important, he used apocalyptic language to describe them.* For example, the passage may have in view a coming invasion of Israel or some other great moment in redemptive history. (Isaiah 13; 24:1-4, 19-23; 30:27-33; Ezekiel 32:2-8; Joel 2:10-11, 28-32; 3:4, 14-17; Amos 5:18-20; 8:9; Zephaniah 1:7, 14-15; Matthew 24-25; Acts 2:14-21.)

a. The Book of Book of Joel is an excellent example of this principle. A coming invasion of the nation is described with vivid apocalyptic imagery. In the "last days," the "day of the Lord" would come and "destruction will come upon them." (1:15) An army of weird locusts will descend upon the nation and strip it clean. While this invasion was not the literal "Day of the LORD" at the End of history, yet, it was so much "like" that Day that it was described as if it were.

b. Joel predicted that "in the last days" the Holy Spirit would be poured out in a dramatic manner not heretofore seen (chapter 2). He used apocalyptic imagery to underscore the importance of this event in the history of redemption.

"And I will show wonders in the heavens and in the earth. The sun will be turned into darkness; and the moon into blood, before the great and the terrible day of the YHWH comes."(Joel 2:30-31)

c. When Peter stated that the above prophecy was fulfilled on the day of Pentecost (Acts 2:16-21), he was not saying that the apocalyptic imagery used by Joel was literally fulfilled on that day. The sun did not literally turn to darkness and the moon into blood on that day. Pentecost was not literarily the "Day of YHWH." The apocalyptic imagery was used to underscore the significance of that day.

2. Jesus used the same technique when He compared His return and the End to Noah's flood, the destruction of Sodom, and the destruction of the temple. While these events did not literally constitute the "End" of the world, yet, they were described as if they were in order to emphasize the catastrophic nature of those events.

3. The failure to understand the use of apocalyptic

language to emphasize important non-apocalyptic events in history has led to two errors.

a. Literalists are left with a host of prophecies that were *not* literally fulfilled. Faced with this fact, some become delusional and pretend that the sun and moon were destroyed at Pentecost! Others invent convoluted principles such as "double" fulfillment. If a prophecy could have two fulfillments then why not three or four fulfillments — or three thousand fulfillments? If a prophecy can mean different things at different times in different places to different people, it means nothing.

b. Preterists fail to understand that just because a future event is described in Scripture with apocalyptic End time imagery; this does not mean that *it* is the End. Something can be *an* "end" (for example: of a city, nation, empire, age, etc.) without being *the* End. In this way, they confuse Pentecost or the destruction of the temple in AD 70 with the End of the world and the return of Christ. The presence of apocalyptic language does not logically or hermeneutically imply that the End is in view. The event may foreshadow the End without being the End itself.

c. Those Preterists who deny a future 2nd Coming of Christ and the Resurrection of the dead by reducing them to some event in history such as Pentecost or the destruction of the Temple, clearly contradict the Seven Ecumenical Creeds of the early Church and the great creeds of the Reformation such as the Westminster Confession. They are thus *not* part of Christian orthodoxy and must be deemed *heretical*. They should be excluded from membership in all orthodox communions. The anathema found in 2

Timothy 2:14-19 is applicable to any form of preterism that denies a future bodily resurrection of the dead at the End.

4. Two things follow from the above observations:

    a.   The mere presence of apocalyptic imagery does not automatically mean that *the* End time is being described.

    b.   We should not automatically assume that a literal fulfillment of apocalyptic images will take place. The imagery could be used to underscore important events not related to the End of history.

5. Do not fall for the silly notion that the issue is whether you take a "literal" or "spiritual" method of interpretation. It is a false distinction that no one really observes.

    a.   Those who teach the dichotomy have never been able to define the words "literal" or "spiritual." Does "literal" mean a real, live dragon or is the dragon a *symbol* for something else? Then we must take a *symbolic* interpretation. But if it is a symbol for some literal person or event, then is it a literal symbol? The definitions end up being absurd.

    b.   The word "literal" establishes a direct correspondence between a word and physical reality. For example, do we interpret the word "dragon" literally or symbolically? A literal interpretation would posit the existence of some kind of huge reptile, perhaps a dinosaur. A symbolic interpretation would deny the existence of this reptile and, instead, would say that the word "dragon" is a symbol for the devil.

c.   Literalists, such as the Dispensationalists, do not *really* believe in literal dragons or a Great Whore riding upon a literal beast. They often give bizarre typological interpretations of such things as the furniture of the tabernacle and generally are as quick to take a non-literal approach as anyone else. Until I see them with one eye gouged out and one hand chopped off, they are full of hot air when they boast that they "take the Bible literally."

d.   Since I have never met anyone who takes a "spiritual" approach to interpreting the Bible, I must assume that this is a straw man invented by literalists as a boogeyman to frighten lay Christians.

6. *It is impossible to decide ahead of time how a passage is going to be fulfilled.* We did a detailed study of all the Old Testament citations in the New Testament to see if there was any way to determine ahead of time how a particular prophecy would be fulfilled. We found no such way.

7. *Each passage must be interpreted in the light of its own layers of context:*

- a word in terms of its grammar, syntax, and vocabulary.

- a verse in the context of the paragraph.

- the paragraph in the context of that Cycle of the chapter.

- that Cycle in the context of the entire chapter.

- that chapter in the context of that Cycle of the book.

- that Cycle in the context of the book as a whole.

- that book in the context of its place in the cannon.

- the historical, cultural, political, and religious context of the author and the people to whom he is writing.

8. *Apocalyptic literature is not the rewriting of past events in order to give them a supernatural twist.* The liberals are hopelessly trapped in a circular argument that since miracles cannot happen, and then predictive prophecies cannot happen. Their anti-supernatural bias is a leap in the dark. It is an example of the psychological phenomenon known as "wish fulfillment." They do not wish miracles to happen, so they don't.

9. *Apocalyptic literature is not a historical narrative of the future.* Read the book of Acts and then the book of Revelation. If you cannot see the difference between historical narrative and apocalyptic writing, you need to take a course in English literature! Apocalyptic literature is not *historical* in nature for the following reasons:

> a. It does not attempt to give the exact names, dates, places, or numbers of End time events, symbols, or images. This is why there are as many interpretations of such things as there are interpreters!

> b. We are told only a *few* of the events to transpire at the End. Thus, we do not have the *whole* picture. Without the entire picture, it is very difficult to interpret the parts.

152

c. Apocalyptic literature is *progressive* in nature with each prophet adding only a few parts of the puzzle. This progress can be seen by comparing Daniel to Revelation. You cannot "stop the clock" by freezing one apocalyptic work such as Daniel and think that you got the whole story.

10. *In apocalyptic literature, the authors used images and symbols from their own personal history and the experience of others to describe the End.* God always revealed His Word to people using their language and their experience so that they could understand what He was saying.

11. *Dress styles (robes, dresses, military uniforms, etc.), modes of transportation (camels, horses, etc.) and military hardware (sword, spears, etc.), are not used in apocalyptic literature as literal predictions that wars at the End will be limited to the clothing, transportation, and military hardware of Ezekiel's day.* Apocalyptic visions such as Ezekiel 38-40 do not mean that the final battle at the End will be done on horseback with swords waving over our heads! It is assumed that the final Battle between good and evil at the End will use whatever clothing, modes of transportation, and weapons that are current at that time.

12. *Since the End would usher in a new form of worship that has yet to be experienced on earth, the authors used contemporary symbols of worship such as temples, priests, and sacrifices because that is all they knew about worship.* It was understood that the use of temple images did not predict that the old Mosaic temple worship would be reestablished on earth in the eternal kingdom after the End. Some literalists have gone so far as to teach that the temple, the Levitical priests, and the

sacrificial system would be established once again. But the book of Hebrews reveals that the temple sacrifices were fulfilled in Christ's death and were done away with. He is now the temple and the tabernacle as well as the Lamb.

13. *Apocalyptic literature used idealized situations from the life experience of the author to paint a beautiful picture of what a wonderful life it will be in the eternal kingdom after the End.* The imagery of everyone sitting under his own tree and just reaching up and picking fruit off his tree whenever he was hungry was not to be taken literally. Neither was the imagery of children playing with poisonous snakes or lions lying down with lambs. The point of such apocalyptic imagery was to emphasize the safe and bounteous life in the eternal kingdom.

14. *In the New Testament, some of the symbols and images of the eternal conscious torment that awaits the wicked at the End were drawn from earlier apocalyptic literature such as 1 Enoch.* It was understood that the fire, the worms, the bottomless pit, the darkness, the dragon, etc. were all *symbols* of something that was so awful that human words could not convey it. No symbol is as real as what it symbolizes. See my book, *Death and the Afterlife* (www.faithdefenders.com) for the documentation for this. To make literal what was originally metaphorical is to make the final Hell less than what it will be.

15. *Apocalyptic literature was free to mix metaphors and symbols because it was assumed that no imagery was to be literally fulfilled.*

    a.   The final hell, Gehenna, could be imagined as a lake of fire and as wandering around in the mist of darkness at the same time because *both* were understood to be *symbols* of the indescribable torment of the damned.

b.   In Matthew 25:31, the earth still exists on the Day of Judgment while in Revelation 20:11 the earth no longer exists. Were the authors contradicting each other? No. It did not matter in apocalyptic literature what symbols or imagery were used because *none* of them were intended to be interpreted literally.

16. *Apocalyptic literature was free to use conflicting chronologies of future events at the End because it was assumed that no chronology was to be taken literally.* It is thus multi-chronological. The attempt to reduce all the different chronologies down to one chronology is nothing more than the old error of reductionism. That this is true is seen from the following illustrations drawn from Scripture.

a.   In the apocalyptic parables of the kingdom found in Matthew 13, Jesus gave the chronology that the *wicked* would be taken *first* and the *righteous left behind* on the Judgment Day (verses 24-30 and 36-43). But in His apocalyptic sermon found in Matthew 24-25, Jesus said that the *righteous* would be taken *first* and the *wicked left behind* (verse 31). Obviously, the wicked and the righteous can't both be first at the same time. One can be first and the other second but they can't both be first.

Was Jesus contradicting Himself? This apparent contradiction can be resolved by the fact that in apocalyptic literature you can have as many conflicting chronologies as you want because *none* of them should be taken as a literal schedule of future events.

b.   According to I Corinthians 15:50-57, the End times events such as the Resurrection, take place "in a moment, in the twinkle of an eye". The words imply that everything will happen instantaneously in a fraction of a second. In other words, it will all be done in an instant. No waiting in line.

Yet, in other apocalyptic passages such as Matthew 25, Revelation 20, etc. the scene is drawn out with Messiah coming to earth; setting up His throne; resurrecting all men; assembling them before His throne for judgment; every one standing in line until his turn to be brought before King Messiah. Then everything we ever thought, said, or did is publicly revealed and judged. Messiah then pronounces judgment upon us and we are either ushered into the eternal kingdom or thrown into the eternal fire.

Now, there is no way this long drawn out apocalyptic vision can be reduced to "in a moment, in the twinkle of an eye." But once it is understood that we are dealing with different apocalyptic visions of the End, then there is no contradiction. None of these things are to be interpreted as a literal calendar of events.

c.   In John 5:25-29, Jesus spoke of the "hour" when "*all* who are in the grave will hear His voice" and come forth, some to life and some to damnation. The passage is straightforward and there is *no* time space between the resurrection of believers and non-believers. The Resurrection is pictured as *a single universal event* embracing *all* of humanity. A-millennialists love this passage and use it to refute Pre-millennialism.

On the other hand, in Revelation 20:4-15, *two* Resurrections with a one thousand year interval between them are pictured. There will be a "first" and a "second" resurrection. The Pre-millennialists, of course, love this passage and use it to refute A-millennialism.

Now, it obvious that John 5 and Revelation 20 confront us with two *different* chronologies of the Resurrection. Is it *one* event or *two* events? Are *all* or only *some* resurrected? They cannot both be *literally* true!

The choice is clear. If we give a literalistic interpretation of John 5 and Revelation 20, the Bible ends up contradicting itself! But if we approach John 5 and Revelation 20 as being *apocalyptic*, then *there is no contradiction because neither passage is to be taken as a literal chronology.*

According to Daniel 12, John 5, I Corinthians 15, Revelation 20, etc. all the dead will be bodily raised and judged by Christ at the End. This much is clear. But when we try to find out the *details* of how and in what order such things will happen, we are *rebuked* in Acts 1:6-7:

> So when they had come together, they were asking Him, saying,
> "Lord is it at this time You are restoring the kingdom to Israel?"
> He said to them, "It is not for you to know the times or epochs

which the Father has fixed by His own authority."

The tense of the verb translated "asking" in verse 6 indicates that they had *repeatedly* asked Jesus about the details of future events. Since this was His last discussion with them before He ascended into heaven, He answered them by pointing that when it came to the details of the future, they were not allowed to know the *chronous* or the *kairos*. Professor F. F. Bruce in his commentary on Acts states,

> "... chronous refers to the time that must elapse before the final establishment of the Kingdom, *karious* to the critical events accompanying its establishment."
> (page 70)

Only the Father knows the details of such things and He has decided *not* to tell us such things.

We must also point out that in the Greek text, the word "not" is taken out of its normal word order in the sentence and put first to reveal that Jesus *stressed* this word. "It is NOT for you to know ..." This grammatical observation underscores the importance of His rebuke.

If we took this passage to heart, there would no pre, post, or a-millennialism. We would be content with the Apostles' Creed:

> He ascended into heaven, and is seated at the right hand of God the Father Almighty; From there He shall come to judge the living and the dead.

> I believe in the Resurrection of the body,
> and the life everlasting. Amen

17. *The failure to understand this is the main error of present day millennial schemes.* They run through the Bible trying to find chronologies to fit their prophetic views.

> a.   The Pre-millennialists seize upon the chronology found in Revelation 20 as the basis for their view. Despite the twin facts that this is the ONLY place in the Bible that refers to a 1,000 year kingdom and it is in a highly symbolic passage with a dragon, an angel, a chain, and a hole in the ground, none of which they view as literal, they demand a literal fulfillment for this chronology.
>
> It never dawns on them that the chronology found in Revelation 20 is only *one of several* different chronologies found in the Bible. Thus, we can admit that Revelation 20 does have a chronology that fits the pre-millennial scheme, but, at the same time, points out that apocalyptic chronologies are not to be taken literally.
>
> b.   The A-millennialists are just as guilty of this error. They grab hold of the chronology found in I Cor. 15 and point out that when Christ returns this means "the End" of His kingdom - not "the beginning" of it. He gives up His kingdom to the Father when He returns.
>
> Since they assume that they must reduce all other biblical chronologies to the one found in I Corinthians 15, they end up giving weird interpretations of Revelation 20.

c.   The Post-millennialists do the same thing with Psalms 22. They think that they have found biblical chronologies that favor their view. In Daniel, chapters 2 and 4, the kingdom grows and covers the earth before the End. But this vision is not intended to be taken as a literal calendar of events. Other passages indicate that the world will be worse at the End, not better!

It is apparent to those who have studied *all* the present prophetic views that they can *all* find apocalyptic chronologies in the Bible to fit their views. Thus they are right and wrong at the same time. *Their failure to understand the genre of apocalyptic literature has doomed them to endlessly squabbling over each other's chronologies.*

18. *The use of Hebrew parallelism and synchronism in which events and things during the same time period are described by several different sets of symbols is a feature of apocalyptic literature that is not well known today.* Imagine one wave of fireworks exploding in the air and then another wave of fireworks shooting up in the same sky. Then another wave and yet another wave of fireworks exploding in the same sky with different colors and symbols. Each wave produced a different pattern in the same space.

a.   This is a good description of what we find in Scripture. For example, in Daniel, the same time period is first described in Nebuchadnezzar's dream of a giant statue in chapter 2 and then described again by the imagery of the four beasts in chapter 7. *The imagery changes but not the time period or the focus.*

160

b.   The book of Revelation is divided into *seven* Cycles that cover the *same* time period but with *different* symbols and imagery each time. If you do not understand this, you would make the mistake of assuming that each set of symbols described a different time period that must be put end to end. For example, the seven seals, the seven trumpets, the seven vials, etc. are not consecutive time periods laid out end to end but the *same* time period with different symbols being used to emphasize different aspects.

c.   Another example is the image of the 144,000 in Revelation 7:4-8. It is then replaced in verse 9 with the image of a crowd that cannot be numbered. Both images are of the *same* group of people seen from different perspectives.

19. *If a symbol in an apocalyptic is explained, do not contradict it or go beyond it.* The symbol of the seven candlesticks in Revelation 1:20 is explained as the seven *churches* of Asia Minor to whom Christ was dictating letters. To claim that the seven candlesticks do *not* present the seven churches but, rather, they refer to seven different consecutive *ages* is to contradict Christ's own explanation!

20. *If a symbol is nowhere explained, then take Paul's advice to heart: "Do not go beyond what is Written" (I Corinthians 4:6).* Once you enter into vain speculations as to the meaning of symbols for which you have no divine interpretation, you can easily fall into a Gnostic attitude in which you imagine that you alone have discovered the secret meaning of a symbol.

21. *In apocalyptic literature, if a symbol is not explained, its meaning is hidden until it is fulfilled.* The

only certain and infallible interpretation of prophecy is its eventual fulfillment in God's timetable. *There is no hermeneutical principle found in Scripture by which we can know ahead of time how and in what way a particular prophecy will be fulfilled.*

Part III

Once we de-apocalypticize biblical prophecy, what do we end up with? You end up where all the creeds of Christianity ended. The do not go into any details. They are not on the side of any modern millennial schemes. They emphasize the core of the biblical vision of the End.

1.   Messiah sits in His resurrected body at the right hand of the Father in heaven.
2.   From there He will personally and literally return to earth.
3.   All men will be resurrected.
4.   He shall judge all men and angels.
5.   He will destroy the old earth by fire and create a new heavens and a new earth where no evil will be allowed.
6.   The elect will inherit the new earth as an everlasting kingdom.
7.   All the demonic and human evildoers shall be locked away in eternal conscious torment in Gehenna.
8.   All things will happen according to God's eternal timetable.

Now, when it comes to detailed questions as to *how* and *in what way* and *in what order* all these events will happen, no one knows. What will be the exact order of events? Are the wicked or the righteous left behind? Who goes first? What kind of resurrection body will we get? Will we look like we do now? If we are radically changed, how will our relatives and friends recognize us? Will we all be young? What age? Is 18 years old a good age? What about 21? Will we all sing like opera stars? Will we all be beautiful, rich, and thin? Or, will such things no longer matter to us at that time because we no longer care about carnal things? Who will be the servants and who will be the people being served? Who hauls away the garbage? Who cleans the streets?

Does everything happen "in a moment, in the twinkle of an eye?" Or, will things get dragged out for years? After all, if everyone is standing in line waiting to be called to judgment, there are a lot of people in front of you! Will the line be arranged alphabetically or by your date of birth or by your date of death?

As a young believer, I was told that I would be called before the throne and Jesus would show my entire life on a big screen so everyone would see everything I ever thought, said, or did, even things done in darkness! As a teenager, this sounded *horrible* to me! The pain and the discomfort felt by the audience who is forced to watch all this stuff is probably as great as the poor person whose life is being exposed to public review! Wouldn't we see icky things that would repulse and sicken us? Who but the most hardened voyeur could bear looking at all the details of every sexual thought, word, and deed of billions of people? Wouldn't this be some kind of pornography?

Those who assume that prophecy is a literal record of future history must answer such questions. Thankfully, the symbols and imagery found in the apocalyptic visions of the Judgment Day are not to be taken literally. There purpose is to emphasize that the Judgment will *complete* and *just*. King Messiah will decide the degree of eternal bliss or torment. Our responsibility is to live each day in the light of the fact that it may be our last day on earth.

> Only one life;

'Twill soon be past.
And only what's done
For Christ shall last.

Conclusion

One of the main purposes of apocalyptic literature is to comfort afflicted and persecuted saints with the assurance that at the End of human history justice shall prevail, the devil will lose, the Messiah will establish his eternal kingdom, the earth will be made into a Paradise once again, and they will be bodily raised immortal and incorruptible.

Apocalyptic comfort gives us the spiritual and psychological strength to go on in the Christian faith and life even when the times are tough and it seems that the forces or evil are winning. At the end of his apocalyptic sermon found in I Corinthians 15, Paul comforted the saints by saying,

> But thanks be to God who gives us the Victory through our Lord Jesus Christ. Therefore, my beloved brethren, be steadfast, immovable, always abounding in the work of the Lord, because you know that your labor in the Lord is not in vain.

Knowing that we are on the winning side gives us the ability to surmount all obstacles and endure all persecution. Keep your eyes on Lord Messiah and the fact that He is coming back one day. Be steadfast, immovable, always abounding in the work of the Lord until you meet Him in heaven at death or in the sky at His return.

Chapter Four

Our Approach

The "Bible" is an encyclopedia of sixty-six ancient Jewish scrolls that were written in different kinds (or genre) of literary styles, in different languages, in different places and times, by different authors, during almost two thousand years. Each genre must be interpreted according to its own unique hermeneutical principles. Thus one hermeneutical principle cannot be applied to all of Scripture. It would be as foolish as attempting to fit all feet into one size shoe. Just as one size shoe does not fit all feet, neither does one hermeneutic fit all of Scripture. For example, there is a great deal of poetry in the Bible.

If we assumed that all Scripture must be interpreted *literally*, then we run into a brick wall in the Psalms. But poetry must be given what we now call "poetic license," i.e. it is not interpreted literally but figuratively. If not, then God is a large chicken because the Psalmist tells us to dwell in the safety of his wings (Psa. 17:9; 36:7; 57:1; 61:4; 63:7; 91:4).

The foolishness of attempting to interpret all Scripture with wooden literalism is the basis of the Mormon doctrine that God was a man with a male body. After all, there are references to God's "hand" and "arm" in Scripture! Are they literal?

This is the same fundamental error of Open Theism. It attempts to interpret Gen. 3:9, 4:9, 11:5, 22:12, etc. in a wooden literalistic manner to mean that God was ignorant and had to ask man to inform him. Thus God did not know where Adam and Eve were hiding or what the tower of Babel was all about or if Abraham loved God. Such foolishness is self-refuting. [12]See our

---

12 See our refutation of "Open Theism" in The Nature and Extent of God's Knowledge (www.faithdefenders.com).

refutation of "Open Theism" in *The Nature and Extent of God's Knowledge* (www.faithdefenders.com).

We begin our study of the Apocalypse with the assumption that it is composed of several literary genres: historical narrative, letters, comments, exhortations, apocalyptic visions, and benediction. Each genre must be interpreted according to its own set of hermeneutical principles. One hermeneutic cannot fit the entire Apocalypse. We have to be pliable enough to switch hermeneutics as the book twists and turns from one genre to another different genre. For example, the poetry, hymns, and doxologies found in the Apocalypse must be interpreted figuratively or we run into all kinds of absurdities.

The historical narratives and biographical Cycles at the beginning, the middle, and the end of the book are meant to be taken literally. John was exiled on Patmos and he was kidnapped by the Messiah and taken on a wild and crazy apocalyptic ride.

Liberal commentators assume that the Apocalypse was actually crafted by John from beginning to end and that he did not actually experience the terrifying visions and sounds described in the book. They will admire John's "genius" in weaving the number seven into the book.

Liberals also assume that John was guilty of a pious fraud in that he pretended that he had visions when he in fact had none. His descriptions of the visions were deliberately crafted to deceive people into thinking that God had revealed the future to him when in fact God did not reveal anything to him.

We believe that the visions John experienced were real. His purpose was not to deceive anyone. It was a straightforward account of what he saw and heard while in an apocalyptic trance.

Sad to say, many conservative commentators assume that John outlined the book before he wrote it. They spend a great deal of time trying to figure out John's preconceived outline or structure that he had in mind as he wrote the Apocalypse.

We do not begin with the assumption that John outlined or pre-structured the book. He did not, in fact, control what he was told to write down, what he saw, and what he heard.

I have a friend who used to take LSD and he claimed that the got more out of the Book of Revelation than straights! During his drug trips, he had uncontrollable visions in which he saw giant spiders and musical notes. He even became a musical note in one of his drug experiences.

While I do not believe that John was eating magic mushrooms or taking drugs, he was experiencing things at such a fast rate that all he could do was record the sounds and sounds as he experienced them. The Apocalypse was *experiential* in the full meaning of the word.

My friend on drugs experienced seeing spiders, while the spiders did not literally exist. In the same way, John experienced seeing a red dragon, while the dragon did not literally exist. *His experience was real to him but what he experienced was neither real nor literal.*

The apocalyptic genre usually has a speaker who experiences heavenly visions, often with trips to heavenly realms, to see and hear mysteries concerning the immediate situation, the near future, and the End of the world (i.e. the resurrection of the dead, the Day of Judgment, and the final bliss and torment awaiting humankind and angels). It arose out of the worldview revealed by God in the Hebrew Scriptures. The following is a summary of the essential elements of Jewish Apocalypticism.

1. The Sovereign God who revealed Himself to the prophets is transcendent above and over time and space and is thus eternal without beginning or end.

2. God is fully omniscient and knows the past, the present, and the future.

3. His knowledge of the future is certain, true, immutable, and infallible because He decreed whatsoever shall come to pass according to the good pleasure of His will.

4. The universe had a Beginning and will have an End.

5. Mankind had a Beginning and will have an End.

6. The Beginning and the End of the universe was predetermined by God and is not the product of chance or luck.

7. The Beginning and the End of mankind was predetermined by God and is not the product of chance or luck.

8. What happens in the universe and human history from the Beginning to the End has been predetermined by God and is not be the product of chance or luck.

9. Since the future history of the universe and mankind is fixed and certain, it can be infallibly and immutably predicted (i.e. prophesied).

10. Since the future can be infallibly and immutably predicted (i.e. prophesied), these predictions can be written down before they happen.

11. The prophecies of Scripture concerning the future will infallibly and immutably happen as predicted (i.e. prophesied).

12. The events that will happen before and during the End have already been predetermined by God and will unfold as He has predicted.

13. God has revealed in Scripture that we cannot know the exact order and timing of the events connected to the End.

14. All our feeble attempts to put the events of the End in some kind of order are only speculative and should not be dogmatized.

15. The events connected to the End are arranged in different orders in Scripture in order to emphasize some aspect of the End, not to give us a literal order of those events.

16. No one can know the day or hour of the End. Thus no one should attempt to set a date for the End.

17. Both the angelic and human righteous are at war against the angelic and human wicked throughout history.

18. God's sovereignty has predetermined that the good will triumph over the wicked and the good will shall live happily ever after.

19. The angelic and human wicked shall suffer eternal conscious torment.

20. In the End, God will be glorified by all things because they were created and ordained to do so.

The Book of Revelation is mislabeled in the KJV as "The Revelation of St. John the Divine." This sad error has misled too many interpreters of the Apocalypse. First, the word "Revelation" does not indicate its unique Jewish nature. It is a Gentile term that does not convey its Jewish meaning.

Second, the words "of St. John the Divine" do not indicate the true author. The inspired title is given in the first verse of the book: "The Apocalypse of Yeshua the Messiah" ('Αποκάλυψις 'Ιησοῦ Χριστοῦ).

The word 'Αποκάλυψις (Apocalypse) tells us that this book is Jewish apocalyptic literature. This means that we cannot interpret this book the same way that we interpret historical narrative (Acts), poetry (Psalms) or didactic (Romans) literature. It will follow different rules.

The words Ἰησοῦ Χριστοῦ (Jesus Messiah) tell us that this book is an apocalyptic work that was dictated by the risen Jesus in his role as the Messiah who brings about the End of the world and judges mankind as predicted in the Scriptures.

This is why we do not accept the idea that the book is actually John's production. He acted as a secretary as Jesus or His angel dictated most of the book.

One of the most important principles of apocalyptic literature is that events are often portrayed in a series of cyclical visions in which the same event is pictured in different ways using different figures or metaphors. Think in terms of a slide carousal that is filled with slides of the same event. One slide comes up while another slide goes down. The carousal has slides of the same event in a cyclical series, not a linear series.

The typical Western European will try to line up apocalyptic visions in a straight line like ducks in a row, assuming that that they are linear, not cyclical. For example, John saw and heard many things in groups of seven:

Seven churches,	Seven bowls,
Seven lamp stands,	Seven kings,
Seven spirits,	Seven angels,
Seven eyes,	Seven mountains,
Seven seals,	Seven judgments,
Seven trumpets,	Seven plagues,
Seven peals,	etc.

These items were arranged into groups of seven not by John, but by the risen Messiah. Out of the hundreds of churches, Jesus selected seven of them to receive a copy of the Apocalypse. That Jesus intended each church to pass their scroll along to other churches is clear from the plural exhortation: "Listen to what the Spirit says to the church*es*" (Rev. 2:7, 11, 17, 29; 3:5, 13, 22).

Westerners assume that these series of sevens should be lined up like ducks in a row, with each referring to a different set

172

of events that take place one after the other in chronology. This is the result of the Western linear mindset. For example, the "seven churches" have been handled differently according to the hermeneutic applied to them. The dispensationalists teach that the seven churches refer to seven successive periods in church history up to the End. They did not actually deal with the present situations of the churches named in the visions. Each generation of dispensationalists claim to be the last stage that will experience the return of Christ.

The Preterists assume that the seven epistles apply only to the seven churches that existed at that time. Thus they are limited to the immediate situation of those churches and have nothing to do with the End.

The apocalyptic approach assumes that each church was chosen by Jesus because it represented one of seven spiritual phases or stages that all local churches and individual Christians go through during their existence. The seven churches with their seven epistles should not be limited to the past or the future. They are repeatable patterns of seven phases in the life of a church or a Christian. All churches and Christians experience all seven phases one time or the other. Thus while the seven epistles directly dealt with the present spiritual condition of each of the seven churches, what is said will be relevant for all churches, because they will all go through all seven stages.

The same holds true for seven seals, seven peals, seven trumpets, etc. Instead of stringing them out in linear fashion, they could be describing in cycles of seven end time judgments what awaits the wicked. They are recapitulations of the same thing over and over again from different perspectives or points of reference. This is why it is so important to keep track of where John is at the time he saw or heard something. Sometimes he is in heaven seeing God's throne and then he is back on earth watching events unfold. Why is this important?

In Rev. 20, he is in heaven where he sees martyred souls sitting on thrones reigning with Messiah in heaven. Thus the "1,000 years" of their reign have to do with a heavenly reign and not with a literal future millennial reign on the earth. Were the thrones heavenly thrones or earthly thrones? They were seen in heaven, not on earth.

This approach is not a new discovery. As a matter of historical record, the earliest extant commentaries on the Apocalypse were written by Christians (Victorinus (A.D. 270) and Tyconius (A.D. 382). They interpreted the Apocalypse as composed of various recapitulations of cycles of visions.

In our study of the Apocalypse, we found that the key verse is found in Rev. 22:8:

> And I, John, am the one who <u>heard</u>
> and <u>saw</u> these things. And when I
> <u>heard</u> and <u>saw</u>, I fell down to
> worship at the feet of the angel who
> <u>showed me these things</u>.

The key words are *"heard"* and *"saw"* that indicate that the book is a series of *audio and visual* presentations of heavenly mysteries. John records what he saw in the following verses:

1:2, 12, 17, 20
4:4
5:1,2, 6
6:1, 9
7:1, 2
8:2
9:1,17
10:1, 5
12:13
13:1, 2, 3, 11
14:6
15:1, 2
16:13
17:3, 6, 8, 12, 15, 16, 18
18:1, 18
19:11, 17, 19
20:1, 4, 11, 12
21:1, 2, 22
22:8

John also recorded when he looked at something:
>4:1
>5:11
>6:2, 5, 8, 12
>7:9
>8:13
>14:1, 14
>15:5

John records what he heard in the following verses:
>1:10
>3:3
>4:1
>5:11, 13
>6:1, 3, 5, 6, 7
>7:4
>8:13
>9:13, 16
>10:4, 8
>11:12
>12:10
>14:2, 13
>16:1, 5, 7
>18:4, 22, 23
>21:3
>22:8

Each new vision and new audio experience marks a new phase or stage in the apocalyptic roller coaster ride that John was on. Each time he sees or hears something new, this marks a new stage.

In our reorganization of the text in chapter one, we emphasized each time the sight or sound changed and he experience something new.

Recapitulations or repetitions occur throughout the book. The scene of the final judgment is repeated:

>6:12-17

7:9-17
11:14-18
14:14-20
15:2-4
16:17-21 16:17 cf. 21:6
17:1-18:24
19:1-10
19:11-21
20:4-6
20:7-15
21:1-8
21:9-22:5

The fall of Babylon is repeated:

14:8;
16:19;
17:16;
18:2, 10, 17, 19-21;
19:2-3.

The earthquake imagery is repeated:

6:12, 14ff;
16:18-20;
20:11.

The final battle is described:

19:17-18, 21;
20:8-9.

Many Christians have been taught that the Book of Daniel is the "key" to the Apocalypse. But this is not completely true. There are many allusions to other prophetic books such as Isaiah, Zechariah, and Ezekiel, and many symbols come from inter-testamental apocalyptic writings.

Whenever I bring up inter-testamental Jewish literature as the source of some of the images found in the Apocalypse, some conservative Christians get nervous and afraid that I am detracting from the authority of Scripture. But this is not a real threat.

The fact that the Bible refers to and at times cites works not found in the Bible only means that those uninspired works contained some correct information. The authors of Scripture did not view these works as inspired. But they were cited because they provided historical information that was accurate. For example, the names of the magicians that opposed Moses are not given in the Pentateuch. Where did Paul give us their names in 2 Tim. 3:8?

> And just as Jannes and Jambres opposed Moses, so these *men* also oppose the truth, men of depraved mind, rejected as regards the faith.

Through the inspiration of the Holy Spirit, he was led to some historical Jewish works that gave him the names of those magicians. Again, when Paul cited from the Greek poets in Acts 17:28, did this mean he viewed them as inspired? Obviously not.

In the same way, that God took cultural and linguistic images drawn from Jewish and Gentile mythology and used them in the Apocalypse should not make us afraid. It does not lessen the infallible nature of Scripture. The symbol of the dragon is found in many ancient cultures and texts. That it was used as a symbol in Jewish Apocalyptic literature only means that the authors wanted to reach the people of their day with symbols they were familiar with.

In my own preaching, I often illustrate sermon points by using contemporary mythologies such as Star Wars, Middle Earth, Narnia, etc. Just because I use one of the battles in Middle Earth to illustrate a point in my sermon does not mean that I believe that the writings of Tolkien are inspired or that Middle Earth actually existed. It only means that Tolkien's mythology has entered our culture and it has supplied us with vivid metaphors for the battle between good and evil.

177

In the same way, when we find contemporary cultural images in the Apocalypse, this does not mean that these things symbolized actually existed. The following illustrations from the Apocalypse demonstrate that God used cultural images drawn from contemporary mythologies.

In Rev. 8:2, we are introduced to a specific group of angels who are described as "the seven angels who stand in the presence of God" (τοὺς ἑπτὰ ἀγγέλους οἳ ἐνώπιον τοῦ θεοῦ ἑστήκασιν).

The definite article (τοὺς) means that the phrase refers to a specific group of angels well known to the readers. Thus, there was no need to explain who they were. Who are they?

There is nothing in Daniel or the rest of the Old Testament to help us identify these seven angels. And there is nothing in the New Testament beyond what is said in the Apocalypse that gives us any clues as to they are. But when we turn to the Jewish literature written between the Testaments, that is where we find several clear references to seven angels that stand in the presence of God.

Since the names and functions of these seven angels had become part of Jewish culture, John and the seven churches knew of them. Thus, there was no need for John to stop and explain who they were. Most conservative scholars have no problem with this fact.

> The article (the seven angels) seems to point to seven well-known angels. In Enoch 20:7 the names of seven archangels are given (Uriel, Raphael, Raguel, Michael, Sariel, Gabriel, Remiel) [13]
>
> Compare the apocryphal Tobit 12:15, "I am Raphael, one of the seven holy angels which present

---

13Robertson, A.T.: Word Pictures in the New Testament. Oak Harbor : Logos Research Systems, 1997, S. Re 8:2

the prayers of the saints, and which go in and out before the glory of the Holy One." [14]

The seven angels who stand before God: these are the seven chief angels, "the Angels of the Presence," who are believed to be continually in God's presence. See Tobit 12.15, "I am Raphael, one of the seven angels who stand in the glorious presence of the Lord, ready to serve him" (TEV); and Luke 1.19, "I am Gabriel ... I stand in the presence of God" (TEV). This is the first time they appear in (Revelation see the seven spirits in front of the throne in 1.4; and verse 4.5)[15]

The seven angels may be identified with the seven well-known archangels of Jewish apocalyptic writings. The article τούς ("the") before ἑπτὰ ἀγγέλους ("seven angels") bears this out (see on 1:4; cf. Tob. 12:15; *1 En.* 20:1–8; 40; 54:6; 71:8–9; 81:5; 90:21–22; *Test. Levi* 3:5; *Pirke de Rabbi Eliezer* 4).[16]

14Jamieson, Robert ; Fausset, A. R. ; Fausset, A. R. ; Brown, David ; Brown, David: A Commentary, Critical and Explanatory, on the Old and New Testaments. Oak Harbor, WA : Logos Research Systems, Inc., 1997, S. Re 8:2

Today's English Version

15Bratcher, Robert G. ; Hatton, Howard: A Handbook on the Revelation to John. New York : United Bible Societies, 1993 (UBS Handbook Series; Helps for Translators), S. 133

16Beale, G. K.: The Book of Revelation : A Commentary on the Greek Text. Grand Rapids, Mich.; Carlisle, Cumbria : W.B. Eerdmans; Paternoster Press, 1999, S. 454

In Rev. 12:2, we find a reference to a seven-headed dragon that is red in color, with ten horns, and seven crowns. There is nothing in Daniel or in the rest of the Old Testament about a Hydra. There is nothing in the New Testament beyond the Apocalypse about a Hydra. But when we turn to the Jewish Apocalyptic literature written between the Testaments, we find references to dragons with several heads who are the symbol of evil and the devil himself.

> *2 Bar.* 29:3–5 says that at the end of time the Messiah will destroy "Behemoth" and "Leviathan … those two great sea monsters." *Test. Asher* 7:3 speaks of God "breaking the head of the dragon in the water," and an early Christian interpolator identified God in this text with Christ in his first coming (likewise, *Testament of Solomon* 12 asserts that a demonic "three-headed dragon" would be "thwarted" by Christ at the cross).[17]

> **A great red dragon.** Homer uses this old word (probably from δερκομαι, to see clearly) for a great monster with three heads coiled like a serpent that ate poisonous herbs. The word occurs also in Hesiod, Pindar, Eschylus. The Babylonians feared a seven-headed hydra and Typhon was the Egyptian dragon who persecuted Osiris. One wonders if these and the Chinese dragons are not race memories of conflicts with the diplodocus and like monsters before their disappearance. [18]

17Beale, G. K.: The Book of Revelation : A Commentary on the Greek Text. Grand

Rapids, Mich.; Carlisle, Cumbria : W.B. Eerdmans; Paternoster Press, 1999, S. 633

18Robertson, A.T.: Word Pictures in the New Testament. Oak Harbor : Logos Research

Systems, 1997, S. Re 12:3-4

The *dragon* was a legendary beast, conceived of as a huge snake, or lizard, and sometimes thought of as living in the ocean depths.[19]

The Ugaritic Baal cycle tells of the battle of Baal, the storm god, with Yam, the prince of the sea. The Babylonians told of Marduk slaying Tiamat, the seven headed monster of the deep. (Marduk's mother was depicted similarly as the woman in 12:1, and Tiamat in battling against heaven is said to have thrown down a third of the stars.) The Persians spoke of the son of Ahura fighting the evil dragon Azhi Dahaka. The Egyptians recounted how the goddess Hathor (Isis, wife of Osiris) fled from the red dragon Typhon to an island; the dragon was overcome by her son Horus and finally destroyed by fire. The Greeks had a similar story in the birth of Apollo from the goddess Leto, who was pursued by the great dragon Python, because he heard that her offspring would kill him. Leto was hidden beneath the sea, and the newly born Apollo immediately attained maturity and slew the dragon. Other variants and additions to the story were current in the Middle East, and some Jews saw in them striking parallels with the promise of the Messiah. An unknown apocalyptic writer took up the saga and adapted it to Jewish hope by adding in v 5 the reference to the male child who is to rule all nations (*cf.* Ps. 2:9) and the defeat of the dragon through

---

19Bratcher, Robert G. ; Hatton, Howard: A Handbook on the Revelation to John. New York : United Bible Societies, 1993 (UBS Handbook Series; Helps for Translators), S. 182

cf. compare

Michael, the guardian angel and protector of Israel (*cf.* Dn. 12:1; there is a remarkable parallel to vs 1–6 in one of the Qumran Hymns of Thanksgiving). It would appear that John was led to set forth the fulfillment of these expressions of pagan belief and OT promise in the Christ of the gospel by the simple addition of vs 10–11, thereby transforming the story into a proclamation of the victory of the crucified and risen Lord over the powers of sin and death. [20]

Jewish tradition elaborated the original figure of a serpent into a dragon with seven heads (see De Wette, p. 127). [21]

That the names of the seven angels mentioned in the Apocalypse come from extra-biblical sources does not mean that the Jewish works that refer to them are inspired. The fact that Messiah used cultural images of contemporary mythology in the Apocalypse does not imply that such creatures existed.

The Outline of the Apocalypse

The following outline follows the stream of consciousness in the visions and sounds that John experienced. It will not satisfy those who want to impose a Western style outline on the book. Our outline follows the twists and turns, ups and downs, and side-to-

---

OT Old Testament

20Carson, D. A.: New Bible Commentary : 21st Century Edition. 4th ed. Leicester, England; Downers Grove, Ill., USA : Inter-Varsity Press, 1994, S. Re 12:1

[21] John Peter, The Revelation of John, (Grand Rapids: Zondervan: n.d.) p. 246.

side movements of John's Holy Ghost apocalyptic roller coaster ride. We let the book take us where it will and are content not to impose an artificial structure on it.

This means we should experience the same confusion that John no doubt experienced. Not everything was explained to him as he was "carried along by the Spirit." And thus no one will be able to explain everything in the book. It will remain a record of heavenly *mysteries.*

Too many Christians have been possessed by a Gnostic lust that craves a "rational" understanding of the future. It is best to remember the cure to such cravings given by Jesus to his own disciples.

> And so when they had come together, they kept asking Him, saying, "Lord, is it at this time You are restoring the kingdom to Israel?" He said to them, "It is not for you to know times or epochs which the Father has fixed by His own authority; but you shall receive power when the Holy Spirit has come upon you; and you shall be My witnesses both in Jerusalem, and in all Judea and Samaria, and even to the remotest part of the earth." (Acts 1:6-7)

In terms of the syntax of the Greek text, the word "not" (Οὐχ) is taken out of its normal word order and placed first in order to emphasize that God is NOT going to feed our lust to know the future. We will just have to trust God that He is in control and that the future will unfold as he has ordained from all eternity.

Jesus counseled them that instead of chasing prophecies, they needed to concentrate on world evangelism (Acts 1:8f). Good advice for all of us.

The Apocalypse was recorded by John, not constructed by him. Let us see what he recorded.

Outline of the Apocalypse from Messiah Jesus

Cycle One

The first Cycle introduces the author of the Apocalypse, its divine Origin, to whom it was written, the focus of the work, and the credentials of the recipient, the key word is "saw."

The Promise of a special blessing to those who read or hear it and its immediate relevance.

The Seven Churches Chosen to receive letters from John

A Salutation from the Holy Trinity.

A Doxology to the Messiah

The First Cycle is closed with the coming of Christ at the end of the world:

John's agreement with the End.

God's agreement with the End.

Cycle Two

The 2nd Cycle takes place on earth and begins with a new introduction:

1st Audio Experience and the seven churches to which the Apocalypse was sent.

1st Vision 2nd Cycle: The Glorified Messiah standing among seven golden lamp stands

Seven descriptions of the glorified Messiah

John's reaction to the vision

Jesus' response to John's fainting: next audio experience

Jesus declares His deity

Time frame of events revealed

Explanation of symbols.

The Letter to the Church in Ephesus

Jesus' exhortation to the Ephesians to receive his letter.

The Letter to the Church in Smyrna

Jesus' exhortation to the Smyrnnans to receive his letter.

The Letter to the Church in Pergamum

Jesus' exhortation for the Pergamumems to receive his letter.

The Letter to the Church in Thyatira

Jesus' exhortation to the Thyatirans to receive his letter.

The Letter to the Church in Sardis

Jesus' exhortation to the Sardists to receive his letter.

The Letter to the Church in Philadelphia

Jesus' exhortation to the Philadelphians to receive his letter.

The Letter to the Church in Laodicea

Jesus' letter to the Laodiceans to receive his letter.

End of Cycle 2.

Cycle Three: visions seen in heaven.

1st Vision in 3nd Cycle:

Audio experience:

185

2nd Vision in 3rd Cycle. John is transported from earth to heaven.

A hymn to the Father

3rd Vision in 3rd Cycle: the Scroll with Seven Seals

4th Vision in 3rd Cycle: The Angel's announcement

5th Vision in 3rd Cycle: the Lamb Takes the Scroll

A heavenly hymn to the Son

6th Vision in 3rd Cycle and next audio experience: the worship of the Lamb

A heavenly hymn to the Son

Audio experience: A universal Doxology to the Father and the Son

7th Vision in 3rd Cycle: the First Seal Opened

Audio experience:

8th Vision in 3rd Cycle: The white horse

9th Vision in 3rd Cycle : the Second Seal Opened

Audio Experience:

10th Vision in 3rd Cycle: the red horse

11th Vision in 3rd Cycle: the Third Seal Opened

Audio Experience:

12th Vision in 3rd Cycle: the black horse

Audio experience:

13th Vision in 3rd Cycle: the Fourth Seal Opened

Audio experience:

14th Vision in 3rd Cycle: the pale horse

15th Vision in 3rd Cycle: the Fifth Seal Opened

Audio experience:

16th Vision in 3rd Cycle:

17th Vision in 3rd Cycle: the Sixth Seal Opened

18th Vision in 3rd Cycle: The Day of Judgment arrives and closes Cycle 3.

Audio experience:

Cycle 3 ends: The End of the world once again described.

Cycle Four

1st Vision in 4th Cycle: four angels, four corners, and four winds

2nd Vision in 4th Cycle: A fifth angel

Audio experience: The 144,000 introduced

3rd Vision in 4th Cycle: The Numberless Crowd

Audio experience: A doxology to the Father and the Son

4th Vision in 4th Cycle:

Audio experience: A doxology to the Father

Audio experience: Explanation of symbol

5th Vision in 4th Cycle: The Paradise that awaits the righteous after the End.

6st Vision in 4th Cycle: the Seventh Seal Opened

7th Vision in 4th Cycle: Seven Angels Given Seven Trumpets

8th Vision in 4th Cycle: A fifth angel with a golden censer

Explanation of symbols:

9th Vision in 4th Cycle:

10th Vision in 4th Cycle:

11th Vision in 4th Cycle: the First Four Trumpets

12th Vision in 4th Cycle: the flying Eagle and new audio experience interrupts Cycle of trumpets.

13th Vision in 4th Cycle: the fifth trumpet, a falling star, a key, the bottomless pit, locust demons, Apollyon.

14th Vision in 4th Cycle: the Sixth Trumpet, the four angels

Audio experience

15th Vision in 4th Cycle:

Explanation of symbols:

16th Vision in 4th Cycle: another Powerful Angel, seven thunders, the small scroll

Audio Experience:

17th Vision in 4th Cycle: The angel makes a vow

Audio Experience:

18th Vision in 4th Cycle: the stick, the temple, the two witnesses, the beast

Explanation of Symbols

19th Vision in 4th Cycle: the Seventh Angel Blows His Trumpet and the End of the world takes place again.

Cycle 4 ends with the Day of Judgment

Cycle 4 ends with the Day of Judgment

Cycle Five

1st Vision of 5th Cycle: the temple opened

2nd Vision of 5th Cycle: A Woman Dressed with the Sun with the moon under her feet

3rd Vision of 5th Cycle: the Red Dragon

4th Vision of 5th Cycle: a War in Heaven breaks out

Explanation of symbols:

Cycle 5 closes with the announcement that the End has come and the kingdom of Messiah has now been set up

Cycle Six

1st Vision of 6th Cycle: the Dragon persecutes the Woman and Her Children

2nd Vision of 6th Cycle: the Beast from the Sea

Exhortation to readers:

3rd Vision of 6th Cycle: Another Beast appears

Seven descriptions of the Beast

4th Vision of 6th Cycle: The powers of the 2nd beast

Explanation of symbols

5th Vision of 6th Cycle: the Lamb and the 144,000 on Mount Zion

Audio Experience: A New Song

6th Vision of 6th Cycle: the first angel preaches the eternal gospel and announces the Hour of Judgment has come

7th Vision of 6th Cycle: A second angel announces the End time judgment of Babylon the Great

8th Vision of 6th Cycle: A third angel announces the End has come.

A Call for Endurance

Audio Experience:

9th Vision of 6th Cycle: the white cloud and the Son of man

10th Vision of 6th Cycle: The fourth angel from the temple

11th Vision of 6th Cycle: The earth harvested

12th Vision of 6th Cycle: Another angel with a sickle.

13th Vision of 6th Cycle: a sixth angel speaks to the fifth angel

14th Vision of 6th Cycle: The fifth angel swings his sickle and throws the enemies of God into the wrath of God.

15th Vision of 6th Cycle: Seven Angels with Seven Plagues bring about the wrath of God to completion

Cycle 6 ends with the Judgment

Cycle Seven

1st Vision of Cycle 7: the Sea of Glass

2nd Vision in Cycle 7: the Temple Opened and seven angels with seven pladgues.

Audio Experience

3rd Vision in Cycle 7: the first angel with the first bowl

4th Vision in Cycle 7: the second angel with the second bowl

5th Vision in Cycle 7: the third angel with the third bowl

Audio Experience

Audio Experience

6th Vision in Cycle 7: the fourth angel with the fourth bowl

7th Vision in Cycle 7: the fifth angel with the fifth bowl

8th Vision in Cycle 7: the sixth angel with the sixth bowl

9th Vision in Cycle 7: Three demonic spirits

Explanation of symbols:

Jesus' exhortation to prepare for his coming

10th Vision in Cycle 7: The demons gather the kings to Armageddon

11th Vision in Cycle 7: the seventh angel with the seventh bowl

Explanation of vision: "It is done"

12th Vision in Cycle 7: the city spilt into three parts

John's comment

13th Vision in Cycle 7: The End of the world; Islands and mountains vanish; mankind is judged;

Cycle 7 ends with the Judgment

Cycle 8 John is now carried to the wilderness

1st Vision in Cycle 8: the judgment of Babylon the Great

2nd Vision in Cycle 8: The Woman rides the beast

3rd Vision in Cycle 8: The Woman drunk with blood

John's comment

Audio experience: The symbols explained by the angel

Audio experience: The angel explains more

4th Vision in Cycle 8: the Fall of Babylon

Audio Experience

Audio Experience

Symbols Explained: The End Judgment has now come upon her

Comment inserted: The reaction of her clients

Audio experience continued

Comments inserted

Comments inserted

5th Vision in Cycle 8: a powerful angel with the millstone

Audio Experience: The End Judgment described.

Audio experience: Cycle 8 closes with the End taking place

Cycle 8 ends with the final judgment.

Cycle 9 begins

John is translated from earth to heaven

1st Vision in Cycle 9: The 24 elders

Audio Experience

Another audio experience

John explains the symbols.

Audio experience starts up again.

John inserts a personal note about his mistake of trying to worship the angel as a warning to his readers.

2nd Vision in Cycle 9: the Second Coming of Christ

3rd Vision in Cycle 9: The Armies of heaven

4th Vision in Cycle 9: the Angel's Gathering of the vultures

5th Vision in Cycle 9: Judgment of the Beast, the False Prophet, and those who followed them

End of Cycle 9 with the final judgment of mankind, the beast and the false prophet by the returning Messiah.

Cycle Ten

The End is recast from the viewpoint of heaven.

1st Vision in Cycle 10: The capture and restraint of the dragon

2rd Vision in Cycle 10: heavenly thrones for those who will judge the earth

3rd Vision in Cycle 10: the souls of martyrs on heavenly thrones.

John's explanation of why they honored.

John explains their reward.

4th Vision in Cycle 10: The fate of the rest of the dead

John inserts an explanation and exhortation

5th Vision in Cycle 10: the freeing and final defeat of Satan, the final battle, and eternal punishment.

6th Vision in Cycle 10: the White Throne Judgment

7th Vision in Cycle 10: heaven and earth vanish

8th Vision in Cycle 10: The dead judged

9th Vision in Cycle 10: a new heaven and a new earth

End of Cycle 10 with the final judgment.

Cycle Eleven

1st Vision in Cycle 11: the holy city descends down from heaven

Audio experience

Another audio experience:

Cycle 11 ends

Cycle Twelve

John is now taken from heaven to view the New Jerusalem.

1st Vision in Cycle 11: The angel show John the Bride of Messiah

2nd Vision in Cycle 12: the Holy City

John describes what he saw:

3rd Vision in Cycle 12: The measuring of the temple

4th Vision in Cycle 12: the River of the Water of Life

Audio Experience

Jesus inserts a promise.

Cycle 12 ends

Epilogue and Benediction by John

John attempts to worship the angel but is corrected.

The Messiah now dictates His concluding words to John.

Audio experience: The Spirit and the Church invites sinners to come to Messiah for salvation.

John warms his readers:

Jesus Speaks:

John's response to Jesus' promise to return: He prays to Jesus and asks him to come back.

John's closing benediction:

Conclusion

This concludes our study of the teaching of the earthly and heavenly Jesus on the End of the World. The Apocalyptic hermeneutic supplies us with a profound way to understand the twists and turns of the last Book of the Bible. One minute we are in heaven, then on earth, then back to heaven, and then back to earth. Strange visions of demonic and angelic beings and cosmic battles between good and evil fill the skies. The four horses of the Apocalypse have been a major theme in Western art and literature. So much blood is shed that it reaches the bridles of the horses. The lake of fire belches out smoke and fire as the antichrist, the false prophet, the devil, and his followers are thrown in alive to be tormented in the presence of the Lamb for all eternity.

The disciples of Messiah can take much comfort from the Apocalypse. It assures them that the good will triumph over evil, Satan and his followers will be defeated in the End, and the righteous will inherit a new heaven and a new earth. The saints can persevere in the faith despite all the trials and persecutions of the devil because they know that their ultimate victory is already predetermined. We thus fight *from* victory, not for victory. May God use this study to renew the excitement that the Apocalypse was intended to inspire.

CPSIA information can be obtained at www.ICGtesting.com
231778LV00002B/152/P